CAMBRIDGE LIBRARY COLLECTION

Books of enduring scholarly value

Archaeology

The discovery of material remains from the recent or the ancient past has always been a source of fascination, but the development of archaeology as an academic discipline which interpreted such finds is relatively recent. It was the work of Winckelmann at Pompeii in the 1760s which first revealed the potential of systematic excavation to scholars and the wider public. Pioneering figures of the nineteenth century such as Schliemann, Layard and Petrie transformed archaeology from a search for ancient artifacts, by means as crude as using gunpowder to break into a tomb, to a science which drew from a wide range of disciplines - ancient languages and literature, geology, chemistry, social history - to increase our understanding of human life and society in the remote past.

Assyria

The Assyriologist George Smith (1840–76) was trained originally as an engraver, but was enthralled by the discoveries of Layard and Rawlinson. He taught himself cuneiform script, and joined the British Museum as a 'repairer' of broken cuneiform tablets. Promotion followed, and after one of Smith's most significant discoveries among the material sent to the Museum – a Babylonian story of a great flood – he was sent to the Middle East, where he found more inscriptions which contained other parts of the epic tale of Gilgamesh. In 1875, he published a history of Assyria for the 'Ancient History from the Monuments' series. Using biblical accounts as well as the Akkadian documents in clay and stone then being excavated in the area, Smith traces the history of the Assyrian empire from its origins until the fall of Nineveh in 612 BCE. Several other books by Smith are also reissued in this series.

T0382207

Cambridge University Press has long been a pioneer in the reissuing of out-of-print titles from its own backlist, producing digital reprints of books that are still sought after by scholars and students but could not be reprinted economically using traditional technology. The Cambridge Library Collection extends this activity to a wider range of books which are still of importance to researchers and professionals, either for the source material they contain, or as landmarks in the history of their academic discipline.

Drawing from the world-renowned collections in the Cambridge University Library and other partner libraries, and guided by the advice of experts in each subject area, Cambridge University Press is using state-of-the-art scanning machines in its own Printing House to capture the content of each book selected for inclusion. The files are processed to give a consistently clear, crisp image, and the books finished to the high quality standard for which the Press is recognised around the world. The latest print-on-demand technology ensures that the books will remain available indefinitely, and that orders for single or multiple copies can quickly be supplied.

The Cambridge Library Collection brings back to life books of enduring scholarly value (including out-of-copyright works originally issued by other publishers) across a wide range of disciplines in the humanities and social sciences and in science and technology.

Assyria

*From the Earliest Times
to the Fall of Nineveh*

GEORGE SMITH

CAMBRIDGE
UNIVERSITY PRESS

CAMBRIDGE
UNIVERSITY PRESS

University Printing House, Cambridge, CB2 8BS, United Kingdom

Cambridge University Press is part of the University of Cambridge.

It furthers the University's mission by disseminating knowledge in the pursuit of
education, learning and research at the highest international levels of excellence.

www.cambridge.org
Information on this title: www.cambridge.org/9781108079068

© in this compilation Cambridge University Press 2014

This edition first published 1875
This digitally printed version 2014

ISBN 978-1-108-07906-8 Paperback

ANCIENT HISTORY

FROM THE MONUMENTS.

ASSYRIA

FROM THE

EARLIEST TIMES TO THE FALL OF NINEVEH

BY

GEORGE SMITH

Of the Department of Oriental Antiquities, British Museum.

PUBLISHED UNDER THE DIRECTION OF
THE COMMITTEE OF GENERAL LITERATURE AND EDUCATION,
APPOINTED BY THE SOCIETY FOR PROMOTING
CHRISTIAN KNOWLEDGE.

LONDON:
Society for Promoting Christian Knowledge.
Sold at the Depositories,
77 Great Queen Street, Lincoln's Inn Fields;
4 Royal Exchange; 48 Piccadilly;
And by all Booksellers.

CLARENDON PRESS, OXFORD.
For the Society for Promoting Christian Knowledge.

PREFACE.

THE following history of Assyria is designed to give some of the results attained from the translations of the Cuneiform inscriptions, which contain the records of the Assyrian empire. Prominence has been given to the incidents of the period when Assyria came in contact with Palestine, and the bearing of some of these is pointed out; but it is rather intended that the reader should compare for himself the history here given from the Assyrian with the parallel account of the Books of Kings. Beside the direct account of persons and events given in the Bible, there is a mass of evidence and illustration on manners and customs, language and literature, tending to throw light on the earlier books of the Bible, which renders the study of Assyrian so important and desirable.

An examination of the dates in this history, will show that many of them do not agree with the authorized system of chronology in the margins of the Bible. Here I must note that, although there is a striking agreement in the order and substance of the events mentioned in both histories, there sometimes appears to be considerable difference as to the dates. As this is an Assyrian history I have taken the dates as they appear to stand in the Assyrian records; but it must be remembered that many of the Assyrian chronological documents are mutilated and incomplete, and that the Assyrians are not always correct in the statements of their histories.

It will be seen by this work that there are great and important periods of Assyrian history of which we know nothing or next to nothing; the reason of which is, that sufficient excavations and researches have not been made on the sites of the Assyrian cities. When Assyria is properly explored, there will no longer be the inequality and uncertainty which even now hangs over so much of her history.

LIST OF THE ASSYRIAN KINGS WITH THEIR APPROXIMATE DATES.

Ismi-dagan	B.C. 1850–1820.
Samsi-vul I	„ 1820–1800.
Igur-kap-kapu } Samsi-vul II	about B.C. 1800.
Ilu-ba } Iritak	about B.C. 1750.
Bel-kapkapu	about B.C. 1700.
Adasi } Bel-bani	about B.C. 1650.
Assur-zakir-esir } Ninip-tugul-assuri	about B.C. 1600.
Iriba-vul } Assur-Nadin-ahi	about B.C. 1550.
Assur-nirari I } Nabu-dan	about B.C. 1500.
Assur-bel-nisisu	B.C. 1450–1420.
Buzur-assur	„ 1420–1400.
Assur-ubalid	„ 1400–1370.
Bel-nirari	„ 1370–1350.
Budil	„ 1350–1330.
Vul-nirari I	„ 1330–1300.
Shalmaneser I	„ 1300–1271.
Tugulti-ninip I	„ 1271–1240.
Bel-kudur-uzur	„ 1240–1220.
Ninip-pal-esar	„ 1220–1200.
Assur-dan I	„ 1200–1170.
Mutaggil-nusku	„ 1170–1150.
Assur-risilim	„ 1150–1120.
Tiglath-Pileser I	„ 1120–1100.
Asser-bel-kala	„ 1100–1080.
Samsi-vul III	„ 1080–1060.
Assur-rab-amar or Assur-rabbur }	about B.C. 1050.
Assur-nimati.	about B.C. 1000.

Assur-dan II	B.C. 930–913.
Vul-nirari II	„ 913–891.
Tugulti-ninip II	„ 891–885.
Assur-nazir-pal	„ 885–860.
Shalmaneser II	„ 860–825.
Assur-dain-pal (rebel king)	B.C. 827.
Samsi-vul IV	B.C. 825–812.
Vul-nirari III	„ 812–783.
Shalmaneser III	„ 783–773.
Assur-dan III	„ 773–755.
Assur-nirari II	„ 755–745.
Tiglath-Pileser II	„ 745–727.
Shalmaneser IV	„ 727–722.
Sargon	„ 722–705.
Sennacherib	„ 705–681.
Esarhaddon	„ 681–668.
Assur-bani-pal	„ 668–626.
Bel-zakir-iskum	„ 626–620.
Assur-ebil-ili	„ 620–607.

List of the Kings of Israel mentioned in the Cuneiform Inscriptions.

Humri	Omri.
Ahabbu	Ahab.
Yahua	Jehu.
Minihimmu	Menahem.
Paqaha	Pekah.
Husia	Hoshea.

List of Kings of Judah mentioned in the Cuneiform Inscriptions.

Azriyahu	Azariah.
Yahuhazi	Ahaz.
Hazaqiyahu	Hezekiah.
Minase	Manasseh.

HISTORY OF ASSYRIA.

CHAPTER I.

COUNTRY AND PEOPLE.

THE extent of Assyria varied from time to time according to the power of the various monarchs, in general increasing from age to age, and reaching its greatest limit about B.C. 650. The original seat of the Assyrians when they migrated from Babylonia [1], was a tract on the river Tigris between latitudes 35° and 37°, a space about 100 miles from north to south, and about seventy miles from east to west. During the best period of the empire, Assyria Proper extended from latitude 35° to 38°, and longitude 40° to 45°, embracing the country on the east of the Tigris to the Median mountains, reaching on the south to below the junction of the rivers Tigris and Zab, on the west extending to the river Khabour and on the north to the mountains of Jebel Djudi. During the seventh century B.C., the subject districts included Lydia, Cyprus, and Egypt on the west, Elam and part of Media on the east, Babylonia and part of Arabia on the south, but in these distant regions the limits of the empire were

---

[1] Genesis x. 11.

uncertain, and the hold upon the provinces only slight.

Assyria Proper is in general flat or with undulating plains, rising only here and there into mountain ranges.

The principal rivers in Assyria, all of which have

Tigris near Nineveh.

a general tendency to run from North to South, are—the Tigris, which passes right through the country and forms the main artery of the district; this river is about 200 yards wide in Assyria, but in the spring during the flood season is very much greater.

The Eastern Khabour, a tributary entering the Tigris on the East, in Northern Assyria; the Great or Upper Zab which joins the Tigris on the same side below Calah [1] or Nimroud ; and the Lower or Lesser Zab, which also joins that river below Assur the old capital of Assyria, are the principal eastern streams.

On the west most of the rivers are small, there being only one of great size, the Western Khabour, formed from the junction of several streams, rising in Mount Masius and flowing southward to its junction with the Euphrates.

Over a considerable part of Assyria the soil is very fertile, and the ground is well adapted for cultivation ; there is excellent clay for brickmaking and pottery, and good building stone ; while the numerous streams give good positions for towns and villages.

The principal cities of Assyria are the following : Nineveh, for a long time the capital of the country, situated on the eastern bank of the Tigris opposite the modern town of Mosul ; Nineveh, which is often mentioned in the Bible, was a city about eight miles round, well fortified and containing a large population.

Kalah [2] or Calah, a large city about twenty miles south of Nineveh, now represented by the mounds of Nimroud Reson a city laying between Calah and Nineveh [3], supposed to be represented by the modern Selamiyeh.

Assur, probably the Rehobothair of Genesis [4], the old capital of the country, represented by the ruins of Kalah Shergat, about sixty miles below Mosul.

---

[1] Genesis x. 11.   [2] Ibid.   [3] Ibid. x. 12.   [4] Ibid. x. 11.

Arbela, modern Ervil, near the eastern mountains, a great centre of Assyrian worship.

The Assyrians who inhabited this region were a race of what we call the Semitic stock, and in character and language allied to the Jews, Syrians, and Arabs. This fact, discovered through the reading of the Assyrian inscriptions, confirms the Scripture genealogies in Genesis x. 21–31, and 1 Chronicles i. 17–23, where the Assyrians, as Shemites, are given as related to the progenitors of the Syrians (Aram), the Hebrews (Eber), and the Arabs (Joktan), all in the Bible called sons of Shem.

The Assyrians had a strength of limb and character, a vigour of mind and body, greater than the other tribes of Semitic descent, and eminently calculated to ensure their ascendency over their weaker neighbours.

The religion of the Assyrians was derived from Babylonia, and very similar to that of the latter country. Both countries worshipped the same deities, but the Assyrians made some changes in the system to give a national character to their pantheon. The principal change made by the Assyrians was the introduction of the worship of Assur, whom they placed at the head of their religion.

Assur, the great god of the Assyrians, was the presiding deity of the city of Assur (Kalah Shergat), and when the Babylonian colonists made that city their capital, its god rose to the position of head of the pantheon. Assur was worshipped as the great god, king of the gods, and father of the gods, and as the Assyrians conceived of him as superior to the other

deities they would not introduce him into the genealogy
of the gods, but called him "The god who created

Assyrian Mythological Figure.

himself." Assur had a famous temple at the city of

Assur called Sadi-matati or "the mountain of the world." This temple was a great place of Assyrian worship, through the whole period of their history.

Among the other principal gods of the Assyrians were—Nebo, whose worship was imported from Borsippa near Babylon. Nebo had a consort named Urmitu; they were the divinities of writing and learning, and are sometimes said to have instructed the Assyrian king like a father and mother. Nebo had a temple at Calah, and another in conjunction with Merodach at Nineveh.

Sin, the moon god, was another deity, and he is generally associated with Shamas or Samas, the sun god. The kings, when under divine protection, are said to have the moon god on the right hand, and the sun god on the left. There was a celebrated temple of Sin at the city of Harran, and one of Shamas at Nineveh.

Merodach, generally worshipped under the name of Bel, is often a companion deity to Nebo. His wife Zirrat-banit is the Succoth Benoth whose worship was set up by the Babylonians transported to Samaria by the king of Assyria [1].

Ishtar or Venus was a favourite object of worship, and had temples at Nineveh and Arbela; in time the Assyrians began to consider the deity worshipped in each of these temples as distinct from the other, and the goddess of Arbela was invested with the character of goddess of war and battle.

Nergal and Ninip, gods of hunting and war; Vul the storm god; Anu king of heaven; and Hea the lord of

---

[1] See 2 Kings xvii. 30.

hell, together with a multitude of minor deities, helped
to fill up the Assyrian pantheon.

The government of Assyria was monarchical, and
the power of the king absolute. He was head of the
army, supreme judge, and viceroy or high-priest of Assur;
but in practice his rule was tempered by the advice of
counsellors, while each department of the state was
directed by competent officers, and there was a regular
code of laws for the administration of the country.

The commander in chief of the army was the
Tartan [1], and there was also a high officer or general
named the rabshakeh [2]. The judges were called dayan;
they decided cases in the gate of the temple or palace;
and there was an appeal from them to the governor
or king. The governors of the various towns were
called sanat or sanuti, they were required to collect and
send up the taxes to the capital, and to furnish every
year the required contingent for the army. The priest-
hood formed a privileged class; they lived on the
revenues of the temples and the offerings of wor-
shippers, while they were directly interested in war, as
a portion of the spoil was dedicated to the temples [3].
The priests used enchantments for removing diseases
and driving away evil spirits, and divination and
astrology were practised before undertaking any
important work.

Various feasts were appointed, but the most remarkable were the "sabbaths," which were in use in Assyria
as well as among the Jews. The Assyrian months
were lunar, and these were divided into four parts

---

[1] 2 Kings xviii. 17.　　　　　　　　　[2] Ibid.
[3] See Numbers xxxi. for a similar custom.

corresponding with the four quarters of the moon, the seventh, fourteenth, twenty-first, and twenty-eighth days, being the sabbaths. On these sabbath days, extra work and even missions of mercy were forbidden, certain foods were not to be eaten, and the monarch himself was not to ride in his chariot. The enactments were similar in character to those of the Jewish Code.

The laws of the Assyrians were arranged and written, and in many respects resembled those of the Israelites and other Oriental nations; a father was supreme in his household, he could expel a child and cut him off from his property, and a similar power was possessed by the wife. If the son or daughter disowned his father he was sold as a slave, and if he disowned his mother he was outlawed. A husband had the power of divorcing his wife on payment of half a manch of silver, and adultery in the woman was punished with drowning.

Slavery was in force among the Assyrians, and whole families were sometimes sold together. There was property in land which in many instances remained in the same family. The Assyrians had a system of leases, so that the land sold returned to its original owners [1], and provisions were made in the leases for alternate crops, in order that the ground might not be impoverished.

The soil of Assyria was generally fertile, and abundant crops of grain were raised; fruit growing and cultivation of flowers were also attended to with success. It was customary for the husbandman to hire

---

[1] See Leviticus xxv.

a field and give as payment one third of the produce of the ground.

The Assyrian army was composed of contingents sent up from the various provincial governors, each government furnishing about 4000 men. These troops met at the capital or at the point of departure for the annual expedition to the number of from 100,000 to 200,000 men, and were composed of swordsmen, spearmen, archers, cavalry, charioteers, &c. The officers were called " saki," and superior officers " rab-saki " (rabshakeh), another rank of commander was called tugalu, and the commander in chief "tartan."

Various trades were practised in Assyria, including weaving, which reached a high state of perfection, dyeing, manufacture of iron, copper, and bronze goods, sculpture and building, ornamental work in stone, metal, wood, &c.

There was a large carrying trade through Assyria, much of which was in the hands of Tyrian merchants [1], and in consideration of the assistance of the king of Tyre, Esarhaddon granted to him a considerable portion of the coast of Palestine. This trade was carried as far as India on the East, and Spain on the West; it passed through Babylon, Nineveh, Carchemesh, and Tyre.

The arts best known from our Assyrian remains are—painting, which was much used in wall decoration; the Assyrian colours being brilliant and well-harmonized, and the effects produced good; sculpture, which was also extensively practised, and reached a

---

[1] Ezekiel xxvii.

high state of perfection; carving in ivory and precious stones; embossing; and ornamental pottery.

Among the pleasures of the people we must give to hunting the first place; the chase of the lion, buffalo, gazelle, wild ass, hare, and other animals, formed a chief amusement of the people, and royal hunts were organized on an extensive scale. Shows and pageants were arranged for the people, and always after a successful war the spoil and ghastly trophies of the victory were paraded through the capital.

The most remarkable feature of Assyrian civilization was their literature and libraries of clay tablets, and it is to these that we owe most of our present knowledge of this great people. The principal Assyrian library was at the capital of Nineveh, and the monarch who did most for Assyrian literature was Assur-bani-pal, the Sardanapulus of the Greeks; to whose time the majority of the tablets belong. As a specimen of Assyrian writing, and at the same time an example of the superstitions of the country, I have translated one of the tablets from Assur-bani-pal's library. This tablet is on the charms to expel evil curses and spells. It is supposed in it that a man was under a curse, and Merodach, one of the gods, seeing him, went to the god Hea his father and enquired how to cure him. Hea, the god of Wisdom, in answer related the ceremonies and incantations, for effecting his recovery, and these are recorded in the tablet for the benefit of the faithful in after times.

Lion Hunt.

Translation of Tablet.

1   The evil curse like a demon fixes on a man
2   a raging voice over him is fixed
3   an evil voice over him is fixed
4   the evil curse is a great calamity
5   That man the evil curse slaughters like a lamb
6   his god from over him departs
7   his goddess stands angry at his side
8   the raging voice like a cloak covers him and bears him away
9   The god Merodach saw him and
10   to his father Hea into the house he entered and said
11   My father, the evil curse like a demon fixes on a man
12   and a second time he spake to him
13   To cure that man I am not able, explain to me how to do it.
14   Hea to his son Merodach answered
15   My son, thou knowest not how, I will recount to thee how
       to do it,
16   Merodach thou knowest not how, I will reveal to thee how
       to do it,
17   what I know, thou shalt know.
18   Go my son Merodach
19   pure . . . . carry to him
20   that spell break, and that spell remove
21   From the curse of his father
22   from the curse of his mother
23   from the curse of his elder brother
24   from the curse of the incantation which the man does not
       know
25   the spell in the words of the lips of the god Hea
26   Like a plant break
27   like a fruit crush
28   like a branch split.
29   For the spell the invocation of heaven may he repeat the
       invocation of earth may he repeat

30   Thus: Like unto this plant which is broken may be the
       spell,
31   in the burning flames it burns
32   in fragments it shall not be collected
33   together or divided it shall not be used
34   its fragments the earth shall not take

35 its seeds shall not produce and the sun shall not raise them
36 for the festival of God and king it shall not be used
37 . . . .
38 the evil invocation, the finger pointing, the marking, the
cursing, the sinning,
39 the evil which in my body, my limbs and my teeth is fixed,
40 like this plant may it be broken and
41 in this day may the burning flames consume,
42 may it drive out the spell and I shall be free

43 Thus: Like unto this fruit which is crushed may be the spell,
44 in the burning flames it burns
45 to its severed stalk it shall not return
46 for the banquet of god and king it shall not be used
47 . . . .
48 the evil invocation, the finger pointing, the marking, the
cursing, the sinning,
49 the evil which in my body, my limbs and my teeth is fixed
50 like this fruit may it be crushed and
51 in this day may the burning flames consume,
52 may it drive out the spell and I shall be free

53 Thus: Like unto this branch which is split may be the spell,
54 in the burning flames it burns
55 its fibres to the trunk shall not return
56 to satisfy a wish it shall not come
57 . . . .
58 the evil invocation, the finger pointing, the marking, the
cursing, the sinning,
59 the evil which in my body, my limbs and my teeth is fixed
60 like this branch may it be split and
61 in this day may the burning flames consume
62 may it drive out the spell and I shall be free

63 Thus: Like unto this wool which is torn may be the spell,
64 in the burning flames it burns
65 to the back of the sheep it shall not return
66 for the clothing of god and king it shall not be used
67 . . . .
68 the evil invocation, the finger pointing, the marking, the
cursing, the sinning
69 the evil which in my body, my limbs and my teeth is fixed
70 like this wool may it be torn and
71 in this day may the burning flames consume
72 may it drive out the spell and I shall be free

73 Thus: Like unto this flag which is torn may be the spell,

74 in the burning flames it burns
75 onto its mast it shall not return
76 to satisfy a wish it shall not come
77 .   .   .   .
78 the evil invocation, the finger pointing, the marking, the
     cursing, the sinning
79 the evil which in my body, my limbs and my teeth is fixed
80 like this flag may it be torn and
81 in this day may the burning flames consume
82 may it drive out the spell and I shall be free

83 Thus: Like unto this thread which is broken may be the
     spell,
84 in the burning flames it burns
85 the weaver into a cloak shall not weave it
86 for the clothing of god and king it shall not be used
87 .   .   .   .
88 the evil invocation, the finger pointing, the marking, the
     cursing, the sinning
89 the evil which in my body, my limbs and my teeth is fixed
90 like this thread may it be broken and
91 in this day may the burning flames consume
92 may it drive out the spell and I shall be free

The clay tablets on which these texts are inscribed are of all sizes from one inch to over a foot long, they are generally covered with Cuneiform characters on both sides, the writing being sometimes so minute that it requires a magnifying glass to read it. Of these there were at least 30,000 in the royal library at Nineveh.

CHAPTER II.

ACCORDING to the tenth chapter of Genesis, the Assyrians were a colony from Babylonia, and first founded the cities of Nineveh, Calah, Rehobothair, and Resen.

In the inscriptions known to us, no account of the origin of Assyria has yet been discovered; but the religion, literature, method of writing, and science, of Assyria, are evidently Babylonian in origin, and agree with the statement of Genesis.

The capital of Assyria in the earliest times was the city of Assur, situated on the western bank of the Tigris, between latitude 35° and 36° and longitude 43° and 44°.

This city was the centre of the worship of the god Assur, after whom the city itself and the country were named, and it is now represented by the mounds of Kalah Shergat.

The government of Assur was at first by patesis or viceroys of Assur, who were subject to Babylonia;

but these, becoming strong, threw off the yoke of the Chaldeans and founded the Assyrian empire.

No details of the earliest period of Assyrian history are known, and we first gain certain knowledge of the country in the nineteenth century B.C., when it was governed by a ruler named Ismi-dagan, and afterwards by his son Samsi-vul, whose date was about B.C. 1820. Samsi-vul built at Assur a temple to the deities Anu and Vul, which was restored 700 years later by Tiglath-Pileser I. Two other rulers of this period are Igur-kapkapu and his son Samsi-vul II. This Samsi-vul built the great national temple to Assur at the capital, and his bricks have been found on the site. A third pair of rulers with similar titles, Ilu-ba and Iritak his son, are known from the inscriptions. Iritak built a temple called "the house of salvation," in memory of some escape of himself and his city. There is no certain information as to the state or power of Assyria at this period, and we only know that the stretch of country governed by them extended from the Lower Zab to above Nineveh, or from about latitude 35° to 37°, for one of the rulers named Samsi-vul repaired a temple at Nineveh, showing that that city was already in existence. It is probable that the territory of Assyria at this time embraced the plain of the Tigris and its tributary streams the Great and Little Zab, and the country already had some importance.

Later Assyrian inscriptions state that the monarchy was founded by Bel-kapkapu, but there is no information as to his age or the extent of his rule.

One of his successors, named Bel-bani son of Adasi,

is said to have been a conqueror, and from him the family of Sargon, the last Assyrian dynasty, claim descent.

The inscriptions supply one or two other doubtful names, but still no real history, until the time of Assur-zakir-esir, who bore the title Lord of countries, and was engaged in some discussions with Babylonia. The discussions between the two countries broke out into war in the time of his successor Ninip-tugul-assuri. This was probably in the sixteenth century B.C., and from this time the country steadily rose in power and importance.

About B.C. 1450 there ruled in Assyria a king named Assur-bel-nisi-su, under whom we begin to know more of the history of the country. The Assyrian and Babylonian monarchs were at this time engaged in treaty as to the boundaries of their respective kingdoms. This discussion was continued under the next king of Assyria, Buzur-assur, about B.C. 1420, and in the reign of Assur-ubalid, king of Assyria about B.C. 1400, the relations between the two countries were cemented by a royal marriage.

Assur-ubalid was a monarch of great renown, his alliance was eagerly sought by surrounding potentates, and he extended the bounds of the empire by war, adding to his territories Subari, on the north of Assyria.

The dominion of the Assyrians now reached to about latitude 38° or higher, extending nearly to Lake Van, on the south to below the lesser Zab, and on the east to about longitude 45°. The western frontier is unknown; but the rule of Assyria probably did not extend to the Khabour at this time. The condition of the countries round Assyria was now favourable to the growth of a large empire, there being no considerable state near Assyria except Babylonia. All the country west of Assyria was open to the inroads of the Egyptians, now in the height of their power. The armies of the Pharaohs in the fifteenth and fourteenth centuries B.C. repeatedly crossed Upper Syria, and sometimes advanced to Nineveh, and although some of the small states occasionally combined against them, there was no power or confederacy in Western Asia able to withstand them. Assyria itself was gradually absorbing the various small states to the north and west, and Assur-ubalid, who enlarged the empire, decorated Nineveh, a city more in the centre of the country than the old capital Assur, which lay too close to the Babylonian frontier. The temple of Ishtar, the goddess of Nineveh, which had been restored by Samsi-vul, had fallen into decay, and was now rebuilt with splendour by Assur-ubalid.

On the death of Assur-ubalid he was succeeded by his son Bel-nirari, who, on the occurrence of a revolution at Babylon, marched into that country and defeated the new party.

Budil, son of Bel-nirari, succeeded his father about B.C. 1350; he was a conqueror, and subdued many peoples in the forest and mountain regions east of Assyria, among these he made tributary the Turuki, Niri, Quti or Goim, Gunuhlami, and Suti. At the capital city, Assur, Budil built a palace, which is the earliest known royal residence in Assyria.

The next monarch was Vul-nirari I, son of Budil,

B.C. 1330, a great ruler, under whom Assyria became the most powerful state of the time. He defeated the Babylonians and extended the empire on the south to Lubdi near the Tigris; and overrunning the district of the Khabour, conquered the Shuites to Rapiqu, a Babylonian city on the Euphrates. On the north he reduced the Subari, who had been previously attacked by Assur-ubalid, and on the east he conquered the Quti and Lulumi. Vul-nirari enlarged the palace at Assur, and restored the causeway to the temple of Assur.

The empire now already included nearly all Assyria Proper and part of Mesopotamia, extending from about longitude 40° to 45° and latitude 35° to 38°.

Shalmaneser I succeeded his father Vul-nirari about B.C. 1300, and continued his conquests; he defeated the Muzri, by whom we may perhaps understand the Egyptians, who were then powerful in Asia, and he conquered the region at the head waters of the Tigris, where he settled an Assyrian colony. The fame of Shalmaneser rests more on his buildings than his conquests; at Assur, the old capital, he enlarged the palace, and restored the great temple called "the mountain of the world." He, however, gave a great blow to the importance of Assur, by founding a palace at Nineveh and making that city a royal residence, and by building a new city about eighteen miles south of Nineveh, which was called Calah. Shalmaneser also restored the temple of Ishtar at Nineveh, and dedicated some votive dishes to the goddess.

On the death of Shalmaneser his son Tugulti-ninip ascended the throne, about B. C. 1271. Under this monarch the Assyrian dominion continued to increase, and war breaking out with Babylonia, the Assyrian king conquered that country and ruled over all the valley of the Euphrates and Tigris, from the Armenian mountains to the Persian Gulf, taking the titles " king of nations, king of Sumir and Akkad, and conqueror of Karduniyas." Tugulti-ninip resided at Nineveh, and further adorned the temple of Ishtar there.

The successor of Tugulti-ninip was named Bel-kudur-uzur, B.C. 1240. In his time the great empire of his predecessor had broken up, and the Babylonian monarch, declaring himself independent, attacked and killed Bel-kudur-uzur.

Ninip-pal-esar succeeded Bel-kudur-uzur B.C. 1220 ; in the midst of these troubles, when the Assyrian power had fallen to a very low ebb, and he had much difficulty in defending himself and re-organizing the Assyrian power, the Hittites and other tribes round Assyria, taking advantage of this period of depression, overran the western and northern provinces, and remained in possession of some parts about a century.

Ninip-pal-esar left his crown to his son Assur-dan I, B.C. 1200, who is said to have had a long and prosperous reign, and who was secure enough in Assyria to make a raid into Babylonia, in revenge for the attacks of the Babylonians on his father. Assur-dan pulled down the temple of Anu and Vul at the city of Assur, which had been built 641 years previously by Samsi-vul; he probably intended to restore it, but died before the commencement of the work.

Mutaggil-nusku, his son, succeeded about B.C.

1170. He rebuilt the palace at Nineveh, but no details are known of his reign.

Assur-risilim, son of Mutaggil-nusku, ascended the throne of Assyria about B.C. 1150. He revived the spirit of conquest in the empire, and defeated the inroads of the Babylonians. The wars of Assur-risilim were principally carried on in the northern and eastern provinces of the empire; here in the mountainous regions which had revolted, he subdued numerous districts, including Ahlami, Lullumi, Quti, Eluni, Matqiu, Suparrun, Ubruhunda, Saga, Sagama, Suria, Hiristu, Andaria, Adavas, and others. The positions of these places are very obscure from the mutilation of the records, and from the fact that the cities were absorbed into the Assyrian empire soon after, and are seldom mentioned. At the close of the reign of Assur-risilim the Assyrian empire nominally extended from below the Lower Zab, about latitude 35°, to Lake Van, then called the Upper Sea. Assur-risilim not only gained fame as a conqueror, but he became also known as a great builder; he rebuilt the palace at Nineveh, and restored the temple of Ishtar with great splendour, placing in it many votive inscriptions.

CHAPTER III.

THE reign of Tiglath-Pileser forms an era in Assyrian history. He subdued the last of the revolting tribes, and continued his father's conquests in every direction, extending the limits of his power from Babylon and Baghdad to the Mediterranean and Lebanon.

Tiglath-Pileser was son of Assur-risilim, and succeeded his father about B.C. 1120. Immediately on his accession he found himself engaged in war. The Muski, an Hittite tribe in Northern Syria, profiting by the late troubles in the Assyrian empire, had overrun the tributary provinces by the Upper Euphrates, and a force of twenty thousand warriors, headed by five kings or chiefs, had conquered and held the districts of Alzi and Puruluz, from which none of the late kings of Assyria had felt strong enough to dislodge them.

On the death of Assur-risilim the Muski advanced into and conquered Kummuha, which lay on both sides of the Euphrates near the sources of the Tigris.

Tiglath-Pileser at once collected his army, and passing the country of Kasiyari entered Kummuha. Here he was met by the forces of the Muski under their five leaders, and overthrew them with considerable loss, on which a large body of the defeated tribe surrendered. Tiglath-Pileser then proceeded to overrun Kummuha, while the people retreated before him and took refuge in the city of Seris, on the river Tigris. This place was attacked and stormed by the Assyrians; Kili-teru the king, his wives and children, with much plunder, fell into the hands of Tiglath-Pileser, who burned the city and destroyed it.

The Assyrian monarch next attacked the city of Urrahinas in the district of Panari, but the people, terrified at the example of Seris, submitted, and Sadi-teru the king took the yoke of Assyria. Tiglath-Pileser received his sons as hostages, and after laying upon Urrahinas a heavy tribute of men, oxen, sheep, and copper, marched to the district of Mildis, a mountainous district, which he ravaged; he then returned to Assyria, where he made rich offerings to his gods, Assur and Vul, from the spoils of the land of Kummuha, which country he annexed to Assyria.

The next expedition of Tiglath-Pileser was to Subari, which he subdued; and he then marched against Alzi and Puruluz, and reduced them to submission. Tiglath-Pileser then resolved to free the province of Subarti, subject to Assyria, which had been conquered by the Hittite tribes of Kaskiya and Urumaya. Four thousand Hittite warriors were encamped in Subarti; but on the approach of Tiglath-Pileser, struck by terror, they all submitted, and gave up to the Assyrians 120 chariots. The Assyrian monarch now again marched into Kummuha, destroying the people and carrying away their goods.

After this Tiglath-Pileser made another campaign in the same direction, and attacked the countries of Haria, Itni, and Aya; from thence he went to Azutappa, where a battle was fought, and the Assyrians took twenty-five cities of Haria, Suira, Itni, Sesu, Arzanibu, Urusu, and Anitku.

Next attacking Adavas, the people fled to the mountains, but afterwards submitted. The two districts of Saravas and Ammavas, which had long before revolted, now felt the power of the Assyrian arms, and were reduced to submission. Isua and Daria were next conquered, and tribute imposed upon them.

Tiglath-Pileser now turned his attention to another portion of his border, and crossing the Lower Zab attacked Muraddas and Saradavas, in Asani and Atuma, south-east of Assyria. Another expedition to the north followed, to the districts of Sugi, Kirhi, Himi, Luhi, Arirgi, Alamun and Elani. From these countries Tiglath-Pileser carried off as trophies twenty-five images of the gods, which he placed in the temples of Beltis, Anu, Vul, and Ishtar.

Passing beyond his northern conquests he now attacked the unsubdued region of Nairi, laying about the Upper Euphrates; the whole of this region is rugged and difficult, but the Assyrian monarch pushed on with great energy, and subdued sixteen districts, carrying his frontier to the Northern Euphrates (the modern Kara-su), about latitude 39°. Stopped here by the barrier of the river, he cut down the forest trees, and made a rough bridge, and passed his army over the Euphrates. Twenty-three of the tribes of the Nairi on the north of the river, alarmed at his approach, gathered their warriors and chariots, and being assisted by sixty petty kings of the neighbourhood, they gave battle to Tiglath-Pileser, who however easily routed them, and pursued the wrecks of their army as far as the Upper Sea. Several of these petty kings fell into the hands of the Assyrians, with chariots, horses, and numerous cattle; and Tiglath Pileser taking hostages from the conquered tribes, fixed upon them a tribute of 1200 horses, and 2000 oxen.

Seni, king of Dayani, one of the principal of these petty sovereigns was taken, and brought prisoner to the city of Assur, but his life was spared by the conqueror, who afterwards restored him to his dominions. Turning from these regions Tiglath-Pileser marched westward to the city of Milidia (modern Malatiyeh), in the district of Hanirabbat; but the people here submitted, and gave at once a present to the king.

After this the Assyrian monarch turned against the region of the Western Euphrates, between the city of Karchemesh and the land of the Shuites; here he ravaged the country, and then crossing the Euphrates on rafts of inflated skins, captured six towns in a region named Bisri.

In his fifth year Tiglath-Pileser marched north of Assyria, beyond the mountain range of Jabel Maklub, where lay a region called Muzur, and a neighbouring country named Qumani. He attacked Muzur and the Qumanians came to their assistance; but both were routed by Tiglath-Pileser, who overran these countries.

Various cities and districts are mentioned, generally of little interest. At one place, Hunasa, Tiglath-Pileser built a fort to secure these conquests, and placed in it tablets of copper, engraved with records of his campaigns.

The later campaigns of Tiglath-Pileser are not so well known, the record not being so complete as the first part of his reign. He afterwards warred in the land of Aram, and the next year attacked the Babylonians; he then continued his ravages in Northern Syria, Kasiyari, Muzri, and on the west of the river Tigris. Tiglath-Pileser also twice more invaded Nairi, and on the third occasion set up a tablet by the sources of the Tigris, recording his conquests, which remains there to this day.

Just before his last expedition to Nairi, Tiglath-Pileser made a grand campaign to the west, which shadowed forth the conquest in this direction of his great successors. He already ruled all the country as far as the Euphrates, and held the two fortresses of Pethor (the birthplace of Baalam) and Mutkinu, on the right of the river; he now marched to Arazigi a city of Syria, and to the foot of the mountains of Lebanon, and reaching the Mediterranean Sea, embarked on its waters in a ship of Arvad and killed a dolphin on the sea. In his war with Maruduk-nadin-ahi king of Babylon, Tiglath-Pileser was at first not so successful, but he afterwards recovered his ground and invaded that country.

Tiglath-Pileser was passionately fond of hunting. He chased wild bulls on the Lebanon, he slaughtered 120 lions, beside numerous other wild animals; and he kept for his pleasure at his capital, Assur, a park of animals of the chase. The king of Egypt knowing his taste, sent an embassy to him, and presented him with a crocodile.

Tiglath-Pileser at the commencement of his reign resolved to rebuild the temple of Anu and Vul, a structure raised by the Assyrian ruler Samsi-vul, 701 years before his time. He restored this temple with great splendour, and raised two towers called ziggurrats, in the shape of pyramids; one of these, now standing, is of great elevation; from it three cylinders were obtained with the records of his exploits. The tomb of Iriba-vul and a memorial mound of Assur-nadiu-ahi king of Assyria he restored. A canal excavated by Assur-dan king of Assyria, to supply the city of Assur with water, had become ruinous thirty years before his time, this he cleaned out and entirely repaired. A raised platform of the palace built by Vulnirari, and a new palace built by Tugulti-ninip he also restored, and he finished the palace at Nineveh commenced by his father Assur-risilim. Various other works were executed by this monarch, who was one of the greatest Assyrian rulers. Tiglath-Pileser left Assyria the foremost monarchy in the world, his empire extending from below the Lower Zab to Lake Van and the Upper Euphrates (Kara-su), and from the mountains east of Assyria to Pethor in Syria, including all the region of the Khabour; while his conquests and expeditions extended on every side outside this line, on the west to the Mediterranean, and on the south to Babylon.

On the death of Tiglath-Pileser, about B.C. 1100,

his crown descended to his son Assur-bel-kala, who is only known by a statue he raised at Nineveh and his war with the Babylonians. He was succeeded by his brother Samsi-vul about B.C. 1080, who restored the temple of the goddess of Nineveh. After his death the Assyrian empire sinks into obscurity, and the very names of its sovereigns are unknown. For a period of 150 years the inscriptions afford us only one ray of light; they record that a disaster overtook the Assyrian arms, the king of Aram (Syria) defeated the Assyrians in the reign of Assur-rabu-amar; Pethor and Mutkinu fell, and with them they lost the whole region of the Euphrates and Nairi.

It is a curious fact that this period of decline in the Assyrian power synchronises with the rise of the Hebrew monarchy. A powerful Syrian empire was founded at Zobah, and David king of Israel having defeated Hadar-ezer king of Zobah, subdued all the kings as far as the river Euphrates. The Jewish power, now under David and Solomon his son, took the place formerly occupied by the Assyrian monarchs; but on the breaking up of this empire on the death of Solomon, the Jews at once lost their supremacy. Western Asia now again consisted of a number of petty principalities, warring against each other, and inviting by their weakness the first invader.

Soon after the death of Solomon, Assyria begins again to emerge into the light under Assur-dan II, the ancestor of a noble line of kings, who reigned about B.C. 940. No military expeditions of Assur-dan are known, but he is recorded to have rebuilt the cities and temples, thus restoring the country

and preparing the way for his successors. Assur-
dan died B.C. 913, and was succeeded by his son
Vul-nirari II, with whom accurate Assyrian chronology begins. Vul-nirari appears to have been a
cruel and successful warrior, and revived the military
power of Assyria, extending the limits of the empire.
On the death of Vul-nirari, his son Tugulti-ninip II
ascended the throne, B.C. 891, and died after a short
reign of six years. He warred in the north in the
district of Nairi, and set up a commemorative tablet
near the sources of the Tigris. At his death in
B.C. 985, his empire extended from below the Lower
Zab across to the Khabour, then north to the region
of Diarbekr, along the south of Lake Van to the
mountains east of Assyria.

At this period during the reign of Vul-nirari II
the Assyrian canon commences its record. This
document contains the names of the officers after
whom the successive years were called, and attached to some of these lists are short statements
of the principal events that happened during these
terms of office, the whole forming a most valuable
body of annual chronology for the best period of
the Assyrian empire.

CHAPTER IV.

Assur-nazir-pal, a warlike and successful monarch, succeeded his father Tugulti-ninip on the throne of Assyria, B.C. 885, and ruled for twenty-five years. As soon as he began to reign he marched against the mountainous district north of Assyria. The country here was divided among numerous petty tribes, who owned their measure of security and independence to the difficult nature of the district in which they resided. The campaign was directed against the district of Elammi and neighbouring places, the cities of Libbe, Surri, Abuqu, Arura, and Arube, near the districts of Urini, Aruni, and Etini. On being attacked the inhabitants fled to the mountains where the Assyrians did not follow them, and Assur-nazir-pal moved off to Kirruri, and took tribute from Kirruri, Simisi, Simira, Ulman, Adavas, Harga, and Harmas, and afterwards, before he left Kirruri, Kirzan and Hupuskia sent a large tribute.

From Kirruri Assur-nazir-pal went to Hulun and Kirhi on the Upper Tigris, here he took various cities and spoiled large districts. A chief named

Bubu, son of Buba, was here captured and carried
to Arbela, where he was flayed alive.

In the year B.C. 884, Assur-nazir-pal went nearly
in the same direction, attacking first the regions of
Niper and Pizatu, on the east of the Upper Tigris;
and then crossing that river into Kummuha, he
received the tribute of Kummuha and Zirki. While
the king stayed in Kummuha, he heard that the
people of the city of Suru by the river Khabour,
had revolted and slain their governor Hamata, and
had raised up a man of Bit-adini, named Ahiyababa
in his stead. Quickly starting his troops Assur-
nazir-pal marched to the Khabour and received the
tribute of Shalmanuha-sar-ilani the ruler of Sadikan
(now Arban). The seal of the grandson of Shalmanuha-sar-ilani is now in the British Museum, and
is one of the most beautiful in the collection.
Passing from Sadikan and Suna, by the banks of
the Khabour, he arrived at Suru, where he captured
Ahiyababa and plundered his palace, and then set
up Azial as governor in his place, Ahiyababa was
brought to Nineveh and there flayed alive. Assur-
nazir-pal now established his authority over the
neighbouring district of Lage, and received tribute
from Hayani of Hindana. After his return from the
Khabour, a potentate who ruled in that neighbourhood, Tlubani, king of the Shuites brought tribute
to Nineveh, and submitted to the Assyrian monarch.

At this time, while he stayed at Nineveh, news
was brought to Assur-nazir-pal that the Assyrians
whom Shalmaneser, a former king of Assyria, had
settled in the city of Halziluha beyond the head

waters of the Tigris, had revolted under Hulai their
chief, and had marched to attack Damdamusa another Assyrian town.

Hearing of this rebellion, B.C. 883, Assur-nazir-pal
marched against the revolters, and on the way came
to a place, near the sources of the Tigris, where
there stood two Assyrian inscriptions carved on the
face of the rock, one of Tiglath-Pileser I the other of
Tiglath-Ninip II; by the side of these Assur-nazir-pal
carved his own image, and then marching against the
rebels, he crossed Kasiyari and came to Kinapu,
a fortress of the revolters, which he took and put
600 men to the sword. Hulai was taken alive and
his skin flayed off, various cities near Kinapu were
punished, and all moveable goods carried away.

From here Assur-nazir-pal moved to Tela, which
he captured and burned. The barbarous customs
of the time are shown by the fact that the Assyrian
monarch cut off the hands and feet, noses and ears,
and put out the eyes of his captives; he then raised
two mounds outside the city, one of human heads,
the other of limbs, and burned the boys and girls
in the fire. Assur-nazir-pal then marched to the
city of Tushan, which he rebuilt and converted it
into an Assyrian station. There had been a famine,
and the Assyrians who had lived there before had
abandoned the place on account of the dearth, and
had gone to Ruri. These were brought back by
Assur-nazir-pal who set them again in Tushan, and
stored grain there against a similar catastrophe.
After this the Assyrian king passed over several
districts near the head waters of the Tigris and

Euphrates, ravaging and burning, and causing scenes
of cruelty similar to those already mentioned.
Next year, B.C. 882, Assur-nazir-pal was called to
the south-east. Zab-vul the chief of Dagara had
overrun the whole of Lamua, and on the borders of
the Assyrian territory near the town of Babite he
had built a fortress as a basis of operations against
Assyria. The king of Assyria moved out to Babite and
there encountered the forces of Zab-vul, who con-
fident in the strength of his army, risked a battle
with Assur-nazir-pal. The forces of Zab-vul were
broken in the conflict, and 1460 of his troops were
slain. Assur-nazir-pal then took Uze, Birutu Laga-
laga and other towns, about one hundred places
being destroyed. This expedition did not settle the
affairs of Lamua, and next year Assur-nazir-pal
started from Kalzi (Hazeh) on the fifteenth day of
Tizri, B.C. 881, and arrived at Babite. From Babite
he went to Nizir of Lullu and Kinipa, and captured
Bunasi the fortress of Muzazina a chief of the district. Following the fugitives, Assur-nazir-pal marched
over the mountains of Nizir, the place famous in the
Chaldean legends as the resting-place of the ark.
Here 326 soldiers were killed and seven cities captured, after which the Assyrian monarch returned to
his camp. Starting out again Assur-nazir-pal invaded
a new part of Nizir which no one before him had
explored, and he captured Larbusa the capital of a
chief named Kirtiari, and eight towns near it. The
whole region was rugged and difficult, and the
mountains are said to have pierced the heavens like

the points of swords. At one time in this expedition, Assur-nazir-pal rode all night in order to surprise a fortress of Zab-vul in the morning.

The war in Lamua still continuing, Assur-nazir-pal again in the autumn of B.C. 881 started from Kalzi, crossing the Lower Zab, and entered the neighbourhood of Babite. He then crossed the river Radanu to the foot of the mountains of Simaki, and after receiving some tribute, crossed the river Turnat to the city of Ammali, the stronghold of a chief named Arastu. This and the places round were captured, and much spoil carried off, and after the conquest of some other petty chiefs, Assur-nazir-pal marched to Kutmar on the borders of Babylonia. Amika of Lamua fled from the Assyrians; and passing on in his victorious course the Assyrian monarch crossed the river Lallu and subsequently the Edir. At every step fresh tribes were met and vanquished, 150 towns were captured, and the expedition closed with the submission of the whole of Lamua.

.While this war was in progress the cities of Hudun, Hartis, Hupuskia, and Kirzan, submitted and sent tribute to Assyria.

These regions being now subdued, Assur-nazir-pal next year, B.C. 880, crossed the Tigris and went to Kummuha, and received the tribute of that region. Passing from thence he went to Yati, and received the tribute of Kirhi; from there he went to Kasiyari, and afterwards invaded Nahiri a second time, and attacked Labturi, son of Tubusi, taking sixty of his towns. Assur-nazir-pal now stopped at Tushan, from there he crossed the Tigris and then rode all night to the city of Pitru a fortress of Dirra. This city was very strong, and surrounded by two walls. Its citadel was on a hill, and looked like the summit of a mountain. On the second day just before sunrise, the Assyrian troops stormed the city, and afterwards burned it with fire. The usual cruelties followed the capture, and 700 of the garrison were impaled round the walls of the town. Many other cities in this region were taken and shared the same fate, and the Assyrian king conquered as far as a place called Arbaki. The city of Arbaki and 250 towns round it fell into the hands of the Assyrian monarch. Assur-nazir-pal now collected the grain plundered in this expedition and placed it in the city of Tushan.

At this time Ammi-bahla a chief subject to Assur-nazir-pal was murdered by his officers, and the Assyrian monarch started out to avenge him, but he was appeased by the gift of a large tribute, and the delivering up of the leader of the revolters, Bur-ramanu, who was flayed alive and his skin exhibited on the wall of Sinapu. Sinapu and other places which had been conquered and colonized by Shal-maneser king of Assyria, had since been taken from Assyria by the Syrians, and now they were restored to the empire by Assur-nazir-pal.

In B.C. 879 the Assyrian king went again to the west; starting from Calah he crossed the river Ti-gris, and then went over to the river Harrit, and from thence to the Khabour, on the banks of which he received tribute from several of the surrounding chiefs; and then descended the Khabour to its junc-tion with the Euphrates, near the city of Hindanu,

and crossing the Euphrates, Assur-nazir-pal halted in
that city. From Hindanu he went to Ilabu, a city
situated on an island in the Euphrates, and from
thence he marched against Suru the capital of Saduda
king of the Suhi. Saduda aware of the expedition
of Assur-nazir-pal, had sent and asked the aid of
Nabu-bal-idina king of Babylonia. He sent a force
to assist the king of Suhi or Shua, and his troops
entrenched themselves in the city of Suru.

Assur-nazir-pal stormed the city, and after two
days' fighting captured it; Saduda and seventy of
his men escaped by swimming over the Euphrates;
and fifty carriages of the Babylonians, Bel-bal-idina
general of the forces, and numerous other prisoners,
fell into the hands of the king of Assyria, who
then plundered the city and set up in it a memorial
of his conquest.

After the return of Assur-nazir-pal to Assyria a
formidable revolt broke out in this region, the Lage,
Hindana, and Shuites, on the west of the Euphrates,
throwing off the yoke of Assyria, crossed the
Euphrates with their troops against him.

Assur-nazir-pal marched against them, and after
laying waste the east of the Euphrates, crossed the
river in boats he constructed on the spot, and re-
conquered these countries from the junction of the
Khabour and Euphrates. In order to hold this
region the Assyrian king founded two cities, one on
the left bank of the Euphrates, called Kar-Assur-
nazir-pal (the fort of Assur-nazir-pal), and one on
the right bank of the river called Nibarti-assur.

In his next campaign Assur-nazir-pal went over new

ground; crossing from Calah the region between the
Tigris and Euphrates, he attacked the territory of
Bit-adini (near the modern Biradjik on the Euphrates).
Kaprabi a strong fortress was captured by the As-
syrians, and then the king of the country Ahuni son
of Adini and Habini king of Tel-abni submitted and
gave tribute. About the year B.C. 870 Assur-nazir-pal made a
great expedition to Syria. Starting on the eighth day
of Iyyar from Calah, he crossed the Tigris to go to
Karchemesh, and touching in his way Bit-bahani,
Azalla, and Bit-adini, received at each place tribute.
Crossing the Euphrates Assur-nazir-pal advanced to
Karchemesh, and Sangara king of Karchemesh the
leading monarch of the Hittites submitted and paid
tribute. Passing out of Karchemesh Assur-nazir-pal
turned his face towards Lebanon, and passing Munzi-
gani and Hamurga, arrived at Hazazi a city of
Dubutna king of the Patina, a tribe living on the
northern part of the river Orontes. Crossing the
river Abre he reached the capital Kunulu, where
Luburna submitted and gave the Assyrian king twenty
talents of silver, one talent of gold, with other articles
of tribute. From Kunulu the Assyrian proceeded on
his course, crossing the rivers Orontes and Sangara,
and passing by the side of Lebanon, he arrived in sight
of the Mediterranean, the great sea, from the shores
of which the Assyrians had been shut out for more
than two hundred years.

While here the great Phoenician trading cities Tyre,
Zidon, Gubal, Arvad, and others, hastened to pay
court and bring rich presents to the conqueror who

had restored the Assyrian power in this direction, and
the Assyrian monarch cut down fine cedars in this
region, and transported them to Nineveh to use in
his buildings.

In the year B.C. 867 Assur-nazir-pal started on his
last expedition. Crossing the Tigris, he advanced to
the country of Kipani and Huziruna, Itti of Azalla
and Giri-dadi of Assaya, gave tribute, and afterwards
Qatizilli of Kummuha submitted ; ascending once
more to the head waters of the Tigris he passed
through Kirhi, Amadani, and Dirri, and arrived at
Amida (now Diarbekr) then held by a chief named
Ilani and passing beyond here, he attacked a chief
named Labturi in the city of Uda, and after destroying
the garrison of the place, annexed it to Assyria.

Assur-nazir-pal rebuilt the palace of Nineveh, and
the temple of Istar at the same place, but he is best
known as the rebuilder of the city of Calah, now
represented by the mounds of Nimroud.

Calah had been founded by Shalmaneser king of
Assyria just above the junction of the Zab with the
Tigris. During the troubles that had since come
over the Assyrian empire the city had been destroyed,
and was in the time of Assur-nazir-pal a heap of
ruins.

The Assyrian monarch resolved soon after his
accession to rebuild the city, and collecting the captives of his various campaigns he brought them to the
site, raised a vast palace mound fronting the Tigris,
600 yards long, and a city about five miles in circumference. This city he peopled with the captives,
and on the palace mound he built two temples and

a palace, from which came some of the best of the Assyrian sculptures in the British Museum.

Assur-nazir-pal also constructed a canal and tunnel from the city of Calah to the river Zab.

Assur-nazir-pal was passionately fond of the chase, and at Calah he kept a preserve of wild animals near the palace.

Assur-nazir-pal appears to have been a ruler of considerable ability, a great warrior, a builder, encouraging the arts and sciences; coming to the throne after a period of depression and inactivity, during which the power of Assyria had been seriously curtailed and her territories reduced, he revived the military power of the empire and again carried the arms of Assyria to Lamua in the east, and to the coast of the Mediterranean on the west. Assur-nazir-pal may be looked upon as the founder of the late Assyrian empire, which from his time gradually increased with but little check, until it reached its greatest limits.

Assur-nazir-pal, after a reign of twenty-five years, was succeeded by his son Shalmaneser II, B.C. 860.

CHAPTER V.

On the death of Assur-nazir-pal he was succeeded by his son Shalmaneser II, about B.C. 860 or 859. The reign of Shalmaneser is historically an important one, because in his time the Assyrians first came in direct contact with the Israelites.

Immediately after he ascended the throne Shalmaneser conducted an expedition to the mountainous region north of Assyria, commencing at Simisi. He first attacked Aridu the capital of a chief named Ninni ; this city he took and destroyed, and while staying there he received tribute from the surrounding districts. Leaving Aridu, Shalmaneser marched to Hupuskia the capital city of Nairi, passing on the way through a rugged mountainous country. The people of Nairi hearing of his advance prepared for resistance, and Shalmaneser burned Hupuskia and the neighbouring cities. Kakia king of Nairi and the remains of his army fled to the mountains, where they were followed and attacked by the Assyrians with great slaughter, their chariots and horses falling into the hands of Shalmaneser; Kakia then submitted to the Assyrian

monarch, who turned from Hupuskia to Suguni, a
fortress of Aram king of Ararat, which he captured,
with fourteen towns in the neighbourhood, then passing to Lake Van, he raised a memorial tablet on its
shore. The country of Ararat now comes forward
in the history; it was at this time becoming civilized,
and adopting among other things the cuneiform mode
of writing. The principal part of Ararat lay on the
north of Lake Van, then called the sea of Nairi. The
king of Gozan, named Azu, now sent tribute to the
Assyrian monarch, consisting of horses, oxen, sheep,
goats and double-humped camels.

In the spring of B.C. 859 Shalmaneser crossed the
Tigris from Nineveh, and passing through the districts
of Hasamu and Dihnum, marched to Lahlahte, a town
of Ahuni son of Adini. Lahlahte was captured by
Shalmaneser, but Ahuni determined to resist the
Assyrians and drew up his forces for battle. Shalmaneser defeated these troops, slaughtering 300 men.
Several of the kings on the east of the Euphrates
now gave tribute, and Shalmaneser passed his army
over the Euphrates on inflated skins, and once more
defeated Ahuni at the city of Pagarruhbuni, slaying
1300 of his troops. Many of the princes on the west
of the Euphrates now submitted, but Ahuni held out,
and calling to his assistance Hani king of Samala,
Sapalulmi of Patina, and Sangara of Karchemesh, they
met Shalmaneser in the land of Samala, and were
routed by the Assyrian forces, after which Shalmaneser
invaded Patina and crossed the Orontes, then passing
to Yazbuk he captured in battle, Burante the king of
the country, and coming in sight of the Mediterranean,

set up a memorial on its shores. In this war we first find Cilicia mentioned, it was then governed by a king named Pihirim. In the year B.C. 858, when Shalmaneser was eponym, he started again to attack Ahuni, and taking the same road, he marched against the city of Tul-bursip on the east of the Euphrates, the capital of Ahuni. Ahuni gave battle to the Assyrians to save his city, but was defeated and forced to cross the Euphrates, closely pursued by Shalmaneser, who proceeded to subdue several of his towns and villages. Passing from thence to the territory of Karchemesh, Shalmaneser laid a heavy tribute on the principal of the surrounding chiefs.

Next year Shalmaneser again marched against Ahuni, who now abandoned the country east of the Euphrates, and crossing to the mountainous region on the west, prepared once more to oppose the Assyrians. The Assyrian monarch now pushed his frontier to the Euphrates, and taking Tul-Bursip, changed its name to Kar-Shalmaneser, settling in this and the neighbouring towns colonies of Assyrians, then crossing the Euphrates again, he recovered the cities of Pethor and Mutkinu, which had fallen into the hands of the Syrians during the decline of the Assyrian empire. Passing to the north-east from the territories of Ahuni, he conquered several small places, and attacked again Aram king of Ararat in his capital Arzasku; Aram, abandoning his city, fled to the mountains, where he was followed by Shalmaneser, who defeated his troops and afterwards wasted the country. Azau of Kirzan and Kaki of Hapuskia were next attacked, and descending by Kirruri the Assyrian monarch re-entered his own territories near Arbela.

In the year B.C. 856 Shalmaneser continued the war against Ahuni, who still held out in a district called Sitamrat, a rugged and difficult country on the west of the Upper Euphrates. Here Ahuni made one more stand against the power that had pressed him for the last four years, and receiving a crushing defeat, he and the whole of his people surrendered to Shalmaneser. The complete subjugation of the kingdom of Ahuni gave the Assyrians a secure hold on the west of the Euphrates and prepared the way for the conquest of Syria and Palestine. This war finished, Shalmaneser the same year carried his troops to the south-east, to Zamua, subduing some petty tribes, and fought a rough naval battle on the waters of a lake.

In his fifth year the Assyrian king marched to the north, to Kasiyari, and took tribute from Ilu-hitti of Rure.

Next year, B.C. 854, Shalmaneser crossed to the region of the river Belichus, to the territories of a chief named Giammu. Giammu was inclined to resist the Assyrians, but his people desired to submit, so they murdered their ruler and surrendered to Shalmaneser, who entered in triumph the cities of Kitlala and Tulsa-abilahi. Passing on to Kar-shalmaneser the Assyrian king crossed the Euphrates there, and received in the city of Pethor the submission and tribute of Sangare of Karchemesh, Kundaspi of Kumuha, Aram son of Gusi, Lalli of Milid, Hayani son of Gabbari, Garparuda of Patina, and Garparunda of Guguma. Leaving the city of Pethor the Assyrians marched to Halman (Aleppo), and there Shalmaneser offered sacri-

E

fices to Vul the god of the city, then ascending the
course of the Orontes he attacked the territory of
Hamath, taking the cities of Adinnu, Barga and Argana.
From Argana Shalmaneser marched to Qarqar (Aroer),
which he captured and burned, but here he was stopped
by a formidable confederacy, Irhulena king of Hamath
having summoned his allies to his assistance.

The leading state in the Syrian league was Damascus,
which had once formed part of the empire of the kings
of Zobah. On the defeat of Hadar-ezer king of Zobah
by David, the Jewish monarch took possession of
Damascus, but the city was afterwards surprised by
Eliadad a Syrian general, and his son Rezon held the
town against Solomon; Rezon was succeeded by his
son Tab-rimmon, and he by his son Ben-hadad I.
Under these kings the dominion of Damascus rapidly
increased, and their power grew so great that Asa
king of Judah sent tribute to Ben-hadad and asked his
aid against Baasha of Israel. Ben-hadad then sent his
army and wasted the north of Israel, and his son
afterwards compelled the submission of Omri king of
Samaria. Ben-hadad II, who ruled at Damascus at
the beginning of the reign of Shalmaneser, is well
known from the account in the Book of Kings of his
wars with Ahab son of Omri. He was ruler of a
confederacy of Syrian states and was the most powerful monarch on the west of the Euphrates. In this
Syrian league the second state was Hamath, and when
Shalmaneser invaded that country he was brought face
to face with the power of Ben-hadad. The troops
brought into the field by the king of Damascus, according to the Assyrian account, consisted of 1200
chariots, 1200 carriages and 20,000 footmen, of

Ben-hadad of Damascus; 700 chariots, 700 carriages
and 10,000 footmen, of Irhulena of Hamath; 2000
chariots and 10,000 footmen, of Ahab of Israel; 500
footmen of the Goim, 1000 Egyptians, 10 chariots
and 10,000 men of Irquanata; 200 men of Matinu-
bahal of Arvad, 200 men of Usanata, 30 chariots and
10,000 men of Adunubahal of Sizana, 1000 camels
of Gindibuh the Arabian, and a force from Bahasha
son of Rehob king of the Ammonites. The whole
force gathered under Ben-hadad probably amounted
to from 80,000 to 90,000 men, and the Assyrian army
was probably about equal in number. The battle
which ensued was obstinately contested, but the advantage lay with the Assyrians, who gradually forced
back their assailants from Aroer to a town named
Kirzan; the contest took place on the banks of the
Orontes, and the river was choked by the wrecks of
the Syrian army; according to one account 14,000
men of Ben-hadad's army were slain, while another
account makes the number 20,500. The Assyrian
army probably also suffered severely, and this battle
put an end to the advance of Shalmaneser in Syria.

In the year B.C. 853, Shalmaneser marched against
Habini king of Tel-abni, and captured and burned his
capital, he then went to the sources of the Tigris, and
carved a tablet in the rock, in which he gives an
account of his triumph over Ben-hadad and the
Syrian league. This tablet is still seen, it is situated
near the town of Egil.

Events in Babylonia now attracted the attention of
Shalmaneser, and he invaded that country in the two
next years, B.C. 852 and 851. The details of these
wars will be given in the history of Babylonia.

In his tenth year, B.C. 850, Shalmaneser again
marched into Syria; four years had elapsed since the
last attack, and in the meantime we know from the
Book of Kings that the Syrian league had been
disturbed by internal wars, and Israel was now at
enmity with the king of Damascus; but Shalmaneser
did not attack them. The Assyrian monarch marched
against the territory of Sangara king of Karchemesh,
and wasted his country, he then entered the dominions
of Aram king of Arne, carrying fire and sword through
the land. While here Ben-hadad and his allies, not
waiting to be attacked, came out and sought the
Assyrians, and another great battle took place. The
engagement was probably less to the advantage of the
Assyrians than the former one, for although Shalmaneser claims the victory he gives no details, and again
his expedition abruptly ended. In the year B.C. 849,
Shalmaneser passed again over the same ground;
crossing the Euphrates he first attacked Sangara of
Karchemesh, and then crossing Yaraku he invaded
Hamath, and captured the town of Astamak with many
smaller places. Once more Ben-hadad of Damascus
and Irhulena of Hamath gathered their hosts to
oppose the Assyrians, and the allies are said to have
suffered a defeat and the loss of 10,000 men. The
resistance opposed by the league was too formidable
to be overcome by the Assyrian army, and so Shalmaneser once more turned north, and attacked the
country of Aram; then marching to Patina received
the tribute of Garparunda the king, and ascending the
mountains of Hamanu cut down trees for building the
temples and palaces of Assyria, B.C. 848. Shalmaneser again crossed the Euphrates, but his operations

were slight, and only consisted of the capture of the city of Paqarhubuna, a place in the mountains. In his thirteenth year the Assyrian monarch marched against the city of the goddesses, in the land of Yatu, an unknown region.

In his fourteenth year, B.C. 846, Shalmaneser made a great effort to conquer Syria, and collecting the whole force of his country, crossed the river Euphrates at the head of 120,000 men, probably the largest army the Assyrians had yet raised. Ben-hadad king of Syria, and the kings who were with him, again came out to battle, and again the Assyrian monarch in the same set phrases claims the victory. Shalmaneser, however, was as far off as ever from the conquest of Syria, at the best he had only gained fruitless victories.

Next year, B.C. 845, Shalmaneser went again to Nairi to the head waters of the Tigris, and in a cave from which the stream issues he carved another memorial of his conquests, then passing a place called Tunabun, he entered the territories of Aram king of Ararat, and marched to the sources of the Euphrates, destroying and burning his towns. While here Asia king of Dayeni submitted to Assyria, and gave tribute.

In his sixteenth year, B.C. 844, Shalmaneser turned his arms in a new direction; crossing the river Zab he invaded the country of Zimri, south-east of Assyria. Maruduk-mudamik the king of Zimri, unable to oppose the Assyrians, fled, and his spoil and gods were carried off to Assyria. Shalmaneser then raised to the throne Yanzu son of Haban.

In the next year Shalmaneser for the first time in

his reign was at peace ; he passed across the Euphrates
to the mountains of Hamanu, and superintended the
cutting of trees for his buildings, but in his course he
met no enemies.

In his eighteenth year, B.C. 842, for the sixteenth
time, Shalmaneser crossed the Euphrates. His purpose
was once more to attack the land of the Hittites, as
the Assyrians called Lower Syria and Palestine. Considerable changes had taken place in those countries
since he first attacked Hamath in his sixth year.
Probably taking advantage of the defeat of Ben-hadad,
at Qarqar, Ahab had broken his alliance with the
Syrian monarch, and had attempted to recover Ramoth-
Gilead, where he was mortally wounded ; and the
death of Ahab had led Mesha the warlike king of
Moab to throw off the yoke of Israel. The various
Syrian kings had likewise broken with Ben-hadad, and
he, after again unsuccessfully besieging Samaria, had
fallen ill and been murdered by Hazael, who had
taken the vacant throne. In Israel the family of Ahab
had been destroyed by Jehu, and a new dynasty
founded at Samaria. Such was the state of the
country when Shalmaneser again turned his arms in
this direction, and advancing to attack Hazael, he
found him without allies or assistance.

Hazael, although abandoned by the neighbouring
princes, resolved on defence, and collecting all his
troops, posted them at a place called Saniru, probably
the Shenir of Scripture. Saniru was situated on one
of the heights before Lebanon, and was an excellent
post for defence. The army of Hazael must have
been very inferior to that of the Assyrians, and when
they joined battle the Syrian monarch was defeated,

with the loss of 16,000 men, 1121 chariots, and 470 carriages, together with the camp of Hazael, fell into the hands of Shalmaneser. Hazael fled from the battle, closely followed by the victors, and shut himself up in his capital, Damascus. Shalmaneser now for

Tribute bearers.   Obelisk of Shalmaneser II.

the first time advanced to besiege the city, and levelled the forests in its vicinity; but finding the work too great he abandoned the siege, and marched into the Hauran, the land of Bashan, wasting the country with fire and sword. Jehu king of Israel, who is called by the Assyrians " Jehu son of Omri," now submitted to Shalmaneser and gave tribute: this, the first tribute of the Israelites to the king of Assyria, is said to have consisted of gold, silver, buckets of gold, cups of gold, and bottles of gold, lead, and rods of wood for maces.

From Hauran the Assyrian monarch marched to Bahlirasi, a place in the mountains, and on the coast of the Mediterranean, where he carved an image of himself in the rock, to celebrate his victories. This was probably at the mouth of the Dog river, the Nahr-el-Kelb, where there are several Assyrian tablets carved in the rock. While at Bahlirasi Shalmaneser received tribute from the two commercial cities of Tyre and Zidon.

Satisfied for the present with the impression he had made on Palestine, Shalmaneser in his nineteenth year, B.C. 841, crossed the Euphrates as usual, but only went up to Mount Hamanu (Amanus), to direct the cutting down of timber for his Assyrian buildings.

Next year, B.C. 840, the Assyrian king crossed the district of Hamanu, and passing on to the land of Que, invaded the territories of Kati; here he carried fire and sword as usual, but without inducing the submission of the country.

In his twenty-first year, B.C. 839, Shalmaneser again directed his forces against Hazael, but that monarch no longer attempted to meet the Assyrian army in the open field, and Shalmaneser marching into his territory, besieged and captured four of his fortresses, then once more passing along to the coast, he took tribute from the Phoenician cities of Tyre, Zidon and Gubal.

Now turning aside from Palestine, in his twenty-second year, B.C. 838, the Assyrian monarch marched to the north west, to the district of Tubal, in Asia Minor. Tubal was then little civilized, and it was governed by twenty-four chiefs or kings. It was a place of great mineral wealth, and here Shalmaneser received the tribute of the chiefs, and visited the mines and quarries.

Next year, B.C. 837, Shalmaneser went in the same direction. Taking in his way the city of Vetas, a fortress of Lalla of Milid, he passed on again to the cities of Tubal and received their tribute.

In his twenty-fourth year, B.C. 836. Shalmaneser turned again to the East, and crossing the Lower Zab,

passed through Hasimir to Zimri. Yanzu king of
Zimri, who had been raised to the throne by the
Assyrian monarch, had revolted, but now fled before
the Assyrian arms. The troops of Shalmaneser took
the cities of Sihisatih, Bit-tamul, Bit-sakki, and Bit-
sedi, and burned them ; then pursuing the people into
the mountains, attacked and destroyed numbers.
From Zimri Shalmaneser went into Persia, which was
then governed by twenty-seven kings, all of whom
submitted ; then he passed on to Media, Arazias, and
Harhar, capturing and destroying many of the towns.

In his twenty-fifth year, B.C. 835, Shalmaneser
crossed the Euphrates, and receiving the tribute of all
the kings of the Hittites, passed across the district of
Hamanu to attack once more Kati king of Que,
besieged and captured the city of Timur, and on his
way back built a palace at the city of Muru, in the
district of Arum son of Agus.

Next year, B.C. 834, Shalmaneser started on his
last expedition over the same ground as the year
before. He first subdued the city of Tanakun held
by a chief named Tulka, then he marched to Lamina
and to the city of Tarzi, and afterwards raised to the
throne Kirri, brother of Kati, the late king of Que
In his return Shalmaneser stayed again in mount
Hamanu to cut timber for transport to Nineveh. On
returning from this expedition Shalmaneser, who had
made twenty-seven campaigns, retired to the city of
Calah for the rest of his life.

In his twenty-seventh year, B.C. 833, Shalmaneser
gathered his army and sent them out from Calah
under command of a trusted general named Dayan-
assur, who was tartan or commander-in-chief of the

Assyrian army, to attack Seduri king of Armenia, who
was organizing a strong power on the north of Assyria. Dayan-assur went to Bit-matzamana, and near
the city of Ammas crossed the river Arzania. Seduri,
king of Armenia, aware of the advance of the Assyrians, came out and risked a battle with them, in
which he was totally defeated.

Soon after this news was brought to Shalmaneser
at Calah that the tribes of the Patina on the Orontes
had killed Luburna their king, and had raised to the
throne Surrila, who was not the legal heir. Again,
B.C. 832, Shalmaneser sent out Dayan-assur in command of his troops, and that general assaulted and
captured Kinalu, the capital of Patina. Surrila committed suicide to avoid falling into the hands of the
Assyrians, and the Patina then submitted. Shalmaneser raised to the vacant throne Sasi, son of Matuzza,
and he delivered up a heavy tribute.

In his twenty-ninth year, B.C. 831, Shalmaneser sent
his general to the head waters of the Tigris, and he
ravaged the district of Kirhi. In the thirtieth year of
Shalmaneser, B.C. 830, Dayan-assur leading out the
Assyrian forces, made an important campaign to the
east, first he crossed the Zab to Hupuskia Daten, the
king submitting and giving tribute; from thence he
went to the cities of Makdabi and Madahir, which
also submitted. From Madahir Dayan-assur went to
Minni. The king of Minni, Udaki, abandoned his
capital city Zirtu and fled, and his country was
pillaged by the Assyrian army. From Minni the Assyrian general marched to the territories of Lusuna
of Harru, capturing his capital Mairsuru. Ardasari
of Surdira was next attacked and submitted; then

the Assyrians marched into Persia, part of the country submitting, those tribes that resisted being ravaged.

In his thirty-first year, b.c. 829, Shalmaneser again sent out Dayan-assur, while he himself performed some religious ceremonies to the gods Assur and Vul. The Assyrian general again marched eastward, passing through Hupuskia, he first attacked the district of Muzazir, south of Ararat or Armenia, taking fifty towns ; he then went on to Kirzan, Harran, Sasgan, and Andia, then carrying his army in a southern direction he attacked the Persians, taking the cities of Bustu, Salahamanu and Kinihamanu, with many smaller places. Afterwards, turning westward, Dayan-assur passed through Zimri, he then marched to the districts of Halman and Simisi and re-entered Assyria.

At this point the annals of Shalmaneser terminate. He reigned until b.c. 825, but the last years of his life were embittered by the rebellion of his eldest son, who took advantage of the age and infirmity of his father to raise the standard of revolt.

On reviewing the reign of Shalmaneser, it is apparent that he was a vigorous warrior and a good general, but he appears to have lacked the power and genius necessary to make the best use of his victories. Most of his wars were carried on in the west, and his first five campaigns were mainly directed against the power of Ahuni, king of Tul-barsip on the Euphrates. When this obstacle was removed, he was stopped until his eighteenth year by the power of the Syrian league, under Ben-hadad, who was by far the greatest enemy he met during his reign. After all his efforts to break the power of this league, on his defeat of Hazael, the Assyrian monarch failed to reap any advantage, and took no further steps to conquer Palestine. It appears to have been the opinion that the empire was extensive enough in this direction, and thus the later campaigns were carried out to the east of Assyria in the countries of Ararat, Minni, Media, and Persia. The Assyrian empire at the close of the reign of Shalmaneser, comprised all the country between the Lower Zab and Lake Van from south to north. On the west it included the region of the Khabour, the Belichus, and Upper Syria to the Mediterranean, and on the east it extended nominally over part of Persia.

Shalmaneser was a great builder, like several other of the Assyrian kings. During his first twelve years he resided at the city of Nineveh, and there he made additions to the palace, which had been rebuilt by his father, and adorned the temple of Ishtar, the goddess of the city. Somewhere about his thirteenth year Shalmaneser changed his capital, and went to reside at Calah, where he ruled for the rest of his life. At Calah he built a new palace south of the one raised by his father, and he completed the building of the city and raising of the walls. At the northern corner of the palace platform at Calah, near the temples, he built an enormous tower or zeggurrat, 167 feet in length and breadth, faced with stone to the height of 20 feet, and still standing 140 feet high.

At the city of Assur, the old capital of the country, the wall having become ruinous Shalmaneser restored it, and greatly strengthened it, which he records on a statue of black stone raised in that city.

On his death, in B.C. 825, this great Assyrian monarch left his crown to his younger son Samsi-vul who had put down the rebellion of his brother.

CHAPTER VI.

THE preference shown by Shalmaneser for the city of Calah, and his holding his court there instead of at Nineveh or Assur, excited the jealousy of the older capitals and caused wide-spread dissatisfaction. The flame of disaffection was fanned by Assur-dain-pal, son of the old monarch, who was impatient to grasp his father's sceptre, and he persuaded the greater part of the country to follow him into revolt, about B.C. 827. The king was old and infirm, there were two princes who were probably to some extent rivals, and the control of the country was in the hands of an aged general, who had been the companion of the monarch in most of his wars.

The cities which followed the lead of the prince, were, Nineveh the capital, on the east of the Tigris, opposite the modern Mosul; this city lost most by the transferring of the capital to Calah, and it headed the revolt. Adia, Sibaniba, an eponym city; Imgurbel and Issapri, Bit-imdir, in a mountainous region; Limu, Siphinis, and Dihnun, between the Euphrates and Tigris; Kipsun, Kurban a place near Nineveh, Tidu, Napulu, and Kapu, Assur, the old capital of the country, Urakka, Salmat, Huzirina, Dur-tila Dariga, and Zab, at the ford of the Great Zab, Lubdi, in the south of Assyria, Arbaha, in the same region, Arbail (Arbela), Amida (Diarbekr), in the north of Assyria, on the Tigris, and Telabni, near the Euphrates, and Hindana, on the Euphrates, near its junction with the Khabour. These twenty-seven great cities, and numerous smaller ones, revolted from Shalmaneser, and proclaimed Assur-dain-pal king of Assyria. The army which remained faithful to Shalmaneser, was placed under the care of Samsi-vul, another son, and this prince re-conquered the various cities, and crushed the rebellion of his brother. Shalmaneser died soon after, and left his crown to his faithful son Samsi-vul, B.C. 825.

The power and influence of Assyria, outside her border, had been lost during the troubles at the close of the reign of Shalmaneser, and the first efforts of Samsi-vul were directed to restoring the former frontiers of the empire.

In his first war, starting for Nahiri, the northern region of Assyria, he swept the whole region, and restored the boundary of Assyria from the city of Padiri, where Minni joins Nahiri, on the north-east of Assyria, to Kar-Shalmaneser on the Euphrates, near the city of Karchemesh. He subsequently restored the southern border from Zaddi, on the borders of Akkad, east of the Tigris along by Aridu, Shua, near the junction of the Euphrates and Khabour, to Bilzi, near Karchemesh.

In his second war Samsi-vul was not personally engaged; he sent a trusted general named Mutariz-assur, who bore the title of rabsaki or rabshakeh.

Mutariz-assur marched to Nahiri, and reached the sea of the setting sun (Lake Van). He captured 300 villages in the territory of a chief named Sarzina, son of Mikdiara, and eleven forts and 200 villages of Uspina, and on his return ravaged the district of Sunba, bringing back much spoil and tribute, including numbers of horses, for which this region was now famous.

The third campaign of Samsi-vul was to the same region; in it he crossed the river Zab, and passed through the district of Zillar, ascending to Hupuskia, the nearest state of Nairi to Assyria. This region submitted, and he received tribute from Dadi king of Hupuskia, Sarzina son of Mikdiara of Zunba, Minni, Persia, and Taurla, principally consisting of horses.

The people of Misu, on the approach of the Assyrians, fled to the mountains, but they were followed and defeated by the army of Samsi-vul, 500 of their villages being destroyed. From Misu Samsi-vul marched to Gizilbunda and captured the city of Kinaki, and crossing some mountains, received the tribute of Titamaska, of Samasa and Kiari of Karsibuta.

The Assyrians destroyed much of Gizilbunda, and Samsi-vul stormed the city of Uras, slaying 6000 men, Pirisati the king, and 1200 men falling alive into his hand. Bel-gur, king of Zibara, now submitted and paid tribute, and the Assyrian monarch carved a statue of himself and set it up in Zibara. From here Samsi-vul went to Media, and the people, on his approach, left their towns and fled to the mountains of Epizi; 2300 men of Hanaziruka the Mede were slain, and 140 carriages beside much spoil taken from him, the city of Sakbita, the royal city, and 1200 villages were taken and spoiled. Turning through Tamuzi, Samsi-vul attacked Arazias, and killed Munirzuarta king of Arazias, and 1070 of his warriors. Many chiefs now submitted, including Sirasmi of Babarur, Amahur of Harmis-anda, Zarisu of Parsani, Zarisu of Hundur, Sanasu of Kipabarataka, Ardara of Ustasa, Suma of Kinuka, Tatai of Gingi-a, Bisira of Arima, Parusta of Kimaru, Aspastatauk of Vila, Amamas of Kingi-istilinzamar, Tarzihu of Maziravus, and many others, all of whom gave tribute, principally horses.

Most of these conquered peoples were Aryan and Turanian tribes, laying east and north of Assyria, and from this time many submitted to the yoke of Assyria, the frontiers being gradually advanced in each direction.

After this, probably about B.C. 810, Samsi-vul came in contact with the king of Babylonia. It appears to have been the design of Samsi-vul to give Assyria a new frontier in this direction. From the earliest ages the frontier between Assyria and Babylonia had passed along on the south of the Lower Zab, but after the wars of Samsi-vul it ran along by the next stream, the Turnat.

On the fifteenth day of Sivan, Samsi-vul crossed the Zab by the cities of Zaddi and Zab, and met in a defile of the mountains three lions, which he hunted and killed, then passing through Ebuh he arrived at the city of Mi-turnat, situated on the river Turnat, this he annexed. He then marched to Garsale, Dihbina, and other places, and later attacked a strong city named Dur-ahisu, which he captured. Alarmed by this inroad, Maruduk-baladsu-ikbi, the Babylonian monarch, collected a large and miscellaneous army of

Babylonians, Chaldeans, Elamites, Zimri, and Arameans, which the Assyrians routed near Dur-ahisu.
Five thousand Babylonians were left dead on the field,
2000 men, 100 chariots, and 200 carriages fell into
the hands of the victor. In the year B.C. 817, Samsi-vul was in the same
region, and annexed the district of Beli.
Next year, B.C. 816, he invaded Zaratu, also in
Babylonia. Continuing these attacks, in B.C. 815 he
marched to Deri, a Babylonian city sacred to a deity
called the great god, and we are told that in this year
there was some procession, or going forth of the great
god at the city of Deri. This festival was repeated
thirty years after, in B.C. 785.
In B.C. 814, Samsi-vul again attacked Babylonia,
reaching Ahsana, and in B.C. 813, he marched to
Chaldea, following this up by taking Babylon in B.C.
812, at the close of his reign. An important historical
document, the synchronous history of Assyria and
Babylonia, was written in the reign of Samsi-vul, and
it appears from this that he obtained the recognition
of a new frontier line, and the cession of the disputed
provinces to Assyria.
No architectural works of Samsi-vul are known,
but he raised two monoliths, one in the city of
Nineveh, in the temple of Ishtar, and the other dedicated to the god Ninip, at the city of Calah. This
last was discovered in the temple of Nebo; it has the
figure of the king in an arched frame, and an inscription in the old hieratic style of Cuneiform writing.
Samsi-vul died in B.C. 812, after a reign of thirteen
years, leaving his crown to his son Vul-nirari, who was
then only a youth.

F

CHAPTER VII.

VUL-NIRARI ascended the throne just after his father's last expedition to Babylonia, he was at the time only a youth, and in his first year did not make any warlike expedition. There are two records of his reign, one a general statement on a pavement slab, the other a notice attached to each year in the eponym canon, stating the country or city to which his expeditions were directed. As these two documents treat his history from entirely different standpoints, it will be necessary to consider them separately, first giving a notice of the slab and then of the canon.

The slab commences with the titles of the monarch, and then gives his conquests, beginning with those at the east; these were Ellipi, the region near Ispahan; Harhar, a region laying between Ellipi and Assyria; this was annexed to Assyria, and a governor appointed over it; Arazias, a district of Media; Misu, a mountainous region in north Media. Media itself is named as conquered; Gizilbunda, a region near Misu; Munna or Minni, a country west of Media; Parsua or Persia, south of Media; Allabri and Abdadana, countries in

this neighbourhood; Nahiri, the region north of Assyria; and Andiu, a place in the further east. On the
west he counts the conquest of the land of the
Hittites, that is of Syria west of the Euphrates, and
all Aharri or Phoenicia, the coast of the Mediterranean, the cities of Tyre, Zidon, the land of Omri,
the kingdom of Israel, Edom, and the Philistines. It
is curious that the kingdom of Judah is the only one
of any importance not included in the list of countries
subject to Assyria at this time. Vul-nirari was reign-
ing at Nineveh during the time of Amaziah king of
Judah and Joash king of Israel.

The only war of Vul-nirari that is given in detail is
one against the king of Syria, and the incidents are
of such interest that it is much to be regretted that
its date is not stated; it is probable, however, from
other sources, that it did not take place earlier than
B.C. 797, and in that year Vul-nirari certainly made
an expedition to Palestine.

Since the war in B.C. 839, when Shalmaneser attacked Hazael, king of Damascus, Syria had been free
from Assyrian inroads. In the meantime Hazael,
and his son and successor, Ben-hadad III, had, by
their inroads, brought the kingdom of Israel to the
verge of ruin, when Jehoash, king of Israel, on his
accession, repulsed the Syrian army, and inflicted three
defeats on Ben-hadad, recovering from him the territory which the Syrians had seized. Ben-hadad, king
of Syria, was now dead, and the government had
descended to the still feebler hands of Mariha, when
Vul-nirari set out on his expedition against Damascus.
Mariha does not appear to have met the Assyrians

in the field, or even stood a siege in his capital, but on the appearance of the army of Vul-nirari, he was overcome by fear, and admitted them within the city; he then made submission, and acknowledged himself a tributary of Assyria, paying in his palace 2300 talents of silver, 20 talents of gold, 3000 talents of copper, 5000 talents of iron, with robes, furniture, and other manufactured articles. Damascus was at this time the richest city and the leading state in Syria, and the submission of Mariha was fatal to the independence of the other states; all were now bound sooner or later to fall under the power of Assyria. After this the Assyrian monarch received the submission of Chaldea, the kings of which gave tribute, and made offerings on the altars of Babylon, Borsippa, and Cutha, for the life of the Assyrian monarch their lord.

The canon history of Assyria contains a short notice of all the campaigns of Vul-nirari, and enables us to fix the dates of his numerous wars.

At the beginning of his reign he does not appear to have made any expedition, but in the year B.C. 810, he commenced his campaigns by invading Media.

B.C. 809.   He invaded Gozau, a region on the river Khabour.

B.C. 808.   Vul-nirari attacked the country of Minni near Lake Urumeya.

B.C. 807.   He marched again into the same region.

B.C. 806.   Vul-nirari commenced a series of attacks on Syria, and went up to Arpad.

B.C. 805.   He marched to Hazazi, near the river Orontes.

B.C. 804. He went to a Phoenician city named Bahali.

B.C. 803. He pushed on to the Mediterranean, and in this year there is said to have been a plague.

B.C. 802. Turning from the west, he invaded Hupuskia, east of Assyria.

B.C. 801. Passing beyond Hupuskia he attacked Media.

B.C. 800. Vul-nirari renewed the invasion of Media.

B C. 799. He invaded the region south-east of Assyria, called Lullumi.

B.C. 798. He marched to the same part against the tribes of Zimri.

B.C. 797. Vul-nirari again invaded Syria, and marched as far as the tribe of Manasseh in Palestine.

B.C. 796. He turned southwards, and invaded Babylonia, passing to Deri.

B.C. 795. He again marched against Deri.

B.C. 794. Vul-nirari invaded Media.

B.C. 793. The king again attacked the same region.

B.C. 792. There was another expedition to Hupuskia.

B.C. 791. Vul-nirari marched against the tribe of Ituha in Babylonia.

B.C. 790. He made another expedition to Media.

B.C. 789. Vul-nirari again went to Media.

B.C. 788. There appears to have been no foreign expedition, but some ceremony or festival took place, by some supposed to be a jubilee.

B.C. 787. Vul-nirari made his last expedition against the Medes.

B.C. 786. There was an expedition to the unknown region of Kibiki.

B.C. 785. There was again war against Hupuskia.

B.C. 784. Vul-nirari at the close of his reign went again against Hupuskia.

Such is a brief statement of the campaigns of this monarch, who appears to have been as vigorous and warlike as his grandfather Shalmaneser. The queen consort of Vul-nirari, who is named with him in one inscription, was Sammuramat or Semiramis, one at least of the queens bearing this name, but it is uncertain if she was the celebrated queen mentioned in the Greek histories. Vul-nirari built a palace at Nineveh, on the mound now called Nebbi-yunas, and he built another at Calah, facing the Tigris, south of the palace of Assur-nazir-pal, and west of that of Shalmaneser.

Vul-nirari also built a temple to the gods Nebo and Merodach, at Nineveh, and another to Nebo at the city of Calah. This last was called Bit-sidda, after the name of the great temple of Nebo at Borsippa in Babylonia; the building was finished and the statues of the gods introduced in the year B.C. 787. Two colossal figures of the god Nebo, standing in a meditative attitude, were placed one on each side of the main entrance of the temple, and four smaller statues with inscriptions were placed in one of the halls of the building. These smaller statues were dedicated by Bel-tarzi-anva, governor of Calah, Hamidi, Musgana, Timina, and Yaluna, to the god Nebo, in gratitude for the saving of his lord Vul-nirari, and his lady the Queen Sammuramat (Semiramis).

Vul-nirari died after a reign of twenty-nine years, and was succeeded by Shalmaneser III, B.C. 783. No memorial of Shalmaneser has come down to us, and the Assyrian canon history is at present the only source of our knowledge of his reign.

On his accession, B.C. 783, he went to Babylonia, to the region of Ituah, on the Euphrates.

B.C. 782. He attacked again the same region.

B.C. 781. Shalmaneser made war with the Armenians, called the kingdom of Ararat. Seduri king of Ararat, during the reign of Shalmaneser II, had introduced Cuneiform writing and various arts into Armenia; and since his time the Armenian monarchy had rapidly risen under his son Ispuni, his grandson Minua, and Argisti the son of Minua. These monarchs had increased the extent of their dominions, making conquests in Syria, Minni, Harhar, Media, and had even made raids into the Assyrian territory. The war now carried on by Shalmaneser against the Armenians appears to have been an obstinate one, and lasted from B.C. 781 through B.C. 780 and 779, closing in the year B.C. 778; then after a short expedition against Ituha, B.C. 777, Shalmaneser again fought with the king of Armenia, B.C. 776. An interval of a year once more followed, Shalmaneser going to Syria, B.C. 775, when again war broke out with Armenia, in conjunction this time with the Zimri, B.C. 774. About this time Shalmaneser died. Six years out of his short reign of ten years had been spent in war with this growing northern power, and at his death the Armenians recommenced their inroads upon Assyria.

Shalmaneser was succeeded, B.C. 773, by Assurdan III, a monarch of whom very little is known.

At the commencement of his reign, B.C. 773, he

attacked Damascus, and the next year went to
Hadrach [1], a town near there.

B.C. 771. Babylonia was invaded and Gannanati
attacked.

B.C. 770. War in the same region followed against
Surat, and B.C. 769, there was another expedition to
Ituha. After this for a year the Assyrian army did
not go out, and then in B C. 767, Assur-dan again
made an expedition to Gannanati, followed in B.C. 766
by one to Media, and B.C. 765 by one to Hadrach in
northern Palestine. Again after this the army rested
at home for a year, and now we begin to see signs of
revolt and disorganization in Assyria itself.

In the year B.C. 763, the old capital Assur became
discontented and revolted, and the same year there
was a remarkable eclipse, which is inserted in the
Assyrian annals, their statement being—"In the
eponymy of Bur-sagale prefect of Gozan the city of
Assur revolted, and in the month Sivan the sun was
eclipsed." This eclipse is a most important event in
several ways, as it is recorded in the Assyrian
chronological canon, under the year which corresponds
to B.C. 763, it formed an excellent test of the accuracy
of the Assyrian record. The eclipse has been calculated by Mr. Hind, and found to have passed over
Assyria at the date indicated in the Assyrian records,
June 15, B.C. 763.

In addition to this Mr. J. W. Bosanquet has pointed
out a remarkable allusion apparently to this eclipse, in
Amos viii. 9, where we read—"I will cause the sun to

---

[1] Zechariah ix. 1.

go down at noon, and will darken the earth in the clear day."

The eclipse of the 15th of June, B.C. 763, passed over Palestine, across Syria and Assyria, and in the latter country appearing when the great city of Assur was in revolt, it was viewed as an evil omen. The revolt in Assur still raged next year, B.C. 762, and in B.C. 761 the flames of disaffection had spread to Arapha, in the south-east, and continued next year, B.C. 760. B.C. 759, the revolt had reached Gozan in the north-west, on the opposite side of the empire. In the sixth year of the revolt, B.C. 758, the Assyrian army marched against Gozan, and crushed out the last embers of this civil war, and Assyria was again a single empire. Assur-dan, however, went out on no new expeditions, and there was a rest of two years, until the death of this prince, B.C. 755.

In the year B.C. 755, Assur-nirari II ascended the throne and made an expedition to Hadrach in North Palestine, and in the next year, B C. 754, he marched to Arpad. After these expeditions a settled decline appears to have taken place in Assyria, and no army went forth for four years; then in the years B.C. 749 and 748, two expeditions marched against Zimri, after which we have again peace. The inaction of the Assyrian monarchs probably caused dissatisfaction in Assyria, and in B.C. 746 a formidable revolt broke out, ending in a change of dynasty; and on the thirteenth day of the month Iyyar, B.C. 745, Tiglath-Pileser II was raised to the Assyrian throne.

CHAPTER VIII.

THE circumstances of the fall of the old dynasty, the revolt at Calah, and the accession of Tiglath-Pileser, we know nothing of, except that Tiglath-Pileser was not related to the royal family. After his accession on the thirteenth day of Iyyar, Tiglath-Pileser set to work to re-organize the kingdom, which had sunk to a low ebb. He at once prepared to meet the enemies who surrounded him on all sides, and in the seventh month, Autumn, B.C. 745, his army was ready, and put in motion to march into Babylonia. Here he had a splendid and successful campaign; he attacked all the tribes of Chaldeans, Arabs, and Arameans about the Euphrates and Tigris, and reduced them to submission; among them were branches of the Nabateans, Hagarenes, Bagdadites, and many others. For some years the power of the kings of Babylonia and Assyria had declined, and the kingdom of Babylon even appears to have been extinct, while the various wandering tribes had increased in power and importance, and their chiefs had encroached on the Babylonian territory in every direction. Now all these tribes were again subdued and rendered tributary to Assyria. All the northern part of Babylonia was also conquered, including Dur-kurigalzu, the city Sippara of Shamas, Kalain, Qurbut, Pahhaz, Kinnipur, and other places, extending to the river Ukni. After this, Tiglath-Pileser set about re-organizing the new territory, and uniting it to Assyria, and on a mound near the Zab, called Tel-hamri, which marked the site of an old city, the Assyrian monarch raised a palace, and round it built a new town, which he filled with people carried off in this expedition. An Assyrian governor was appointed, and a garrison told off for the city, which Tiglath-Pileser called the city of Kar-assur, or the " fort of Assur." These operations extended and secured the southern frontier of Assyria, and showed Tiglath-Pileser to be a vigorous ruler, with the ability to restore the power of Assyria.

In his second year, B.C. 744, the attention of the new monarch was directed to the east of Assyria. The last two military expeditions of the Assyrian army, before the accession of Tiglath-Pileser, were directed against the land of Zimri; but this region was always lawless and unsettled, and took advantage of any opportunity to throw off the Assyrian yoke.

Zimri was now overrun by Tiglath-Pileser, who attacked Bit-sangibuti, Bit-hamban, Sumurzu, and numerous other places, and wholly subdued the region, then pouring his troops across the eastern frontier of Zimri, he attacked the Persians and conquered many of their tribes, and reached what was called the gold region of Media. Everywhere the cities were attacked, tribute

demanded, and people and spoil carried off, rulers and
people abandoned their cities and fled, others submitted
and paid tribute, a few resisted and were destroyed, but
nowhere could any barrier be raised against the successful march of the Assyrian army, and Tiglath-Pileser
returned to Assyria, his army flushed with success and
bringing 50,500 prisoners, with numerous herds of
horses, oxen, sheep, and other animals. Tiglath-Pileser
endeavoured to secure these conquests, and appointed
Assyrian governors in several of the cities and districts,
but most of the territory returned to independence as
soon as the Assyrian army had gone home.

As a supplement to his own campaign, Tiglath-
Pileser sent a general named Assur-dain-ani, who was
rabsaki and governor of Mazamua, to subdue eastern
Media, and he marched to a region named Bikni bringing back much spoil. The exploits of Tiglath-Pileser
now attracted the attention of the various monarchies
north and west of Assyria. These regions had for
some years been free from Assyrian inroads, but it was
evident that their turn would come, so some of them
who were more immediately exposed made alliances
against the Assyrian monarch. The leading state in
one of these alliances was Ararat or Armenia, the
monarch of which bore the name of Sarduri. Sarduri
made alliance with Sulumal of Milid (Malatya), Tarhulara of Gauguma, Matihil son of Agus, and Kustaspi
(Hystaspes) king of Kummuha, and they collected a
formidable force which they posted in the vicinity of
Kastan and Halpi, in the country of Kummuha. This
confederacy in northern Syria and Armenia barred the
way against the Assyrians and shut them out of Syria,

Tiglath-Pileser therefore at once accepted the challenge
and advanced against Kummuha, where he totally
routed the army under the leadership of Sarduri, B.C.
743. Sarduri fled from the battle-field on a mare by
night, and crossing the bridge over the upper Euphrates,
escaped into his own territory. The bulk of the army
and stores appear to have fallen into the hands of
Tiglath-Pileser, who captured 72,950 soldiers, with the
state carriage and royal chariot of. Sarduri, his neck-
lace, his state palanquin, horses, asses, and a vast spoil.

Tiglath-Pileser did not follow Sarduri; but now that
the way was opened, crossed the Euphrates and advanced into Syria and entered the city of Arpad. All
the kings of Upper Syria now sent to Arpad, and gave
tribute to Tiglath-Pileser, who at once re-established the
influence of Assyria as far as Tyre and Samaria. The
princes who acknowledged his power and gave tribute,
were Kustaspi of Kummuha, who had just been defeated by Tiglath-Pileser; Razanu (Rezon) of Damascus,
the leading state in Syria, on him a heavy tribute
was imposed, including eighteen talents of gold, beside
silver and other things; Minihim (Menahem) of Samaria, this name is not in the list, which is now
mutilated, but he most probably gave tribute, as his
name is inserted in later copies; Hiram of Tyre,
Uriyakki of Qua, Sibitti-bahali of Gubal, Eniel of
Hamath, Pisiris of Karchemesh, Tarhulara of Gaugama, and Panammu of Samhala. Most of these
princes ruled in northern Syria, between the Euphrates
and the Mediterranean, and their submission gave
Tiglath-Pileser the control of the country as far as
the sea.

After the Assyrian army had retired, the kings of
Syria appear to have repented of their hasty sub-
mission, and fortifying Arpad, they revolted against
Assyria.

Tiglath-Pileser had now a severer task before him,
and in the spring of B.C. 742 he crossed the Euphrates
and invested the city of Arpad, the stronghold of the
Syrians. Here he met with an obstinate resistance,
and the siege of the city lasted through the year. In
B.C. 741 Tiglath-Pileser again came up and found his
army still encamped before this fortress, which held
out until B.C. 740, when the Assyrians captured it.

The fall of Arpad once more brought northern
Syria to the feet of Tiglath-Pileser, and he now
marched against Tutamu king of Unqi, who had taken
advantage of these troubles to revolt against Assyria.
Kunali the capital of Tutamu was captured and destroyed, Tutamu and his great men being captured.
The whole country was plundered, and then reduced
to an Assyrian province, Kunali being rebuilt and an
Assyrian governor placed in it. The submission of
the Syrian kings in B.C. 740 was again only for a brief
period, and Tiglath-Pileser had to lead out his army
once more in this direction in B.C. 739, he at the same
time directed part of his force against the north, where
the influence of Armenia was still great, in spite of the
recent defeat of Sarduri; here he attacked and conquered Birtu on the Euphrates, Ulluba and Kirhu east
of that river, and the district of Kullimir, where he set
up a memorial of his conquests.

In Palestine a new power was interfering in the
affairs of Assyria. Azariah king of Judah, one of the

most warlike of the descendants of David, had formed
an alliance with Hamath against Assyria, and the
people of Hamath had revolted against Tiglath-Pileser.
The Assyrian monarch was equal to the occasion, and
on his arrival in Syria, began step by step to reconquer
the rebels. One of the marked events of the war was
the capture of the city of Kullani, the Calno of Isaiah
x. 9, to the capture of which Sennacherib alludes in
his message. After the capture of Calno, B.C. 738, a
way was once more opened for Tiglath-Pileser to
overrun Syria, and he struck at the confederacy headed
by Azariah king of Judah. He defeated their forces,
and then proceeded to reconquer the kingdom of
Hamath. The cities of Uznu, Siannu, and many others
near the sea, Bahali-zabuna (Baalzephon) Ammana
(Amana) and various places near Lebanon and Hadrach
near Damascus.

Tiglath-Pileser then parcelled out the land of Hamath
among his generals, annexing nineteen districts to
Assyria. While Tiglath-Pileser was conquering in
Syria, his generals were equally fortunate in other
directions. The Aramean tribes on the banks of the
Euphrates and Tigris had broken out into rebellion;
one of his generals quelled this revolt, and captured
the cities of Birtu-sa-kiniya and Sarragitu, he then led
12,000 prisoners, with many flocks and herds to Tiglath-
Pileser, in Syria. The governor of Lullumi invaded
the region east of the Tigris, and capturing the city of
Mulugani, and the surrounding places, brought his
prisoners to Tiglath-Pileser. The governor of Nahiri
took the city of Suburgillu and other places, and
brought captive to Tiglath-Pileser a chief named Sigila
and numerous captives.

The Assyrian monarch now transported numbers of the captives taken in these wars into other countries; 1223 people of Hamath, were transported to the head waters of the Tigris. 600 women of Amlate, Damuni, and Dur, places in Babylonia, were sent into Kunalia, Hazarra, and various other places in Unqi, a number of women of the Guti and Sangibuti, together with 1200 men of the Illili and 6200 of the Nakkip and Buda, were placed in Simirra, Arga, and various other cities of Hamath, near the sea, 578 men of Buda and Duna and various other tribes of captives were placed in the city of Tuhammi, while more of the people of Guti and Sangibuti were placed in Tulgarmi. It is evident from the lists, that the men from one district were mixed with the women from another, with a view to the destruction of national feeling and the fusion of the races into the Assyrian empire.

These conquests and changes wrought by Tiglath-Pileser were brought to a fitting termination, by his receiving the tribute of all the kings of Syria, and some of those in Palestine. This list includes the names of Kustaspi of Kummuha, Rezon of Syria, Menahem of Samaria, Hiram of Tyre, Sibitti-bahali of Gubal, Urikki of Qua, Pisiris of Karchemesh, Eni-il of Hamath, Panammu of Samala, Tarhulara of Gauguma, Sulumal of Milid, Dadilu of Kaska, Vassurmi of Tabal (Tubal), Ushitti of Tuna, Urpalla of Tuhana, Tuhammi of Istunda, Urimmi of Husinna, and Zabibe queen of the Arabs.

The tribute brought to Tiglath-Pileser by these sovereigns consisted of gold, silver, lead, iron, skins and horns of oxen, dyed garments of flax and wool, various woods, dyed wool, birds of beautiful plumage, horses, oxen, sheep, camels, she-camels and young, and other things, being the best products of the countries.

The next year, B.C. 737, Tiglath-Pileser started again for the east, and passing through Zimri, invaded Media; Tiglath-Pileser passed over nearly the same ground, and·captured the same cities as in his second expedition. He met with resistance from Upas son of Kipsi, who collected his forces to oppose the Assyrians, but these were obliged to fly, and their cities were burned. Bur-dada a neighbouring chief also fled, but was pursued and captured by the Assyrians. After numerous other chiefs and tribes had been subdued, Tiglath-Pileser came to a city founded by the Assyrians, called Tel-assur, and devoted to the worship of the god Merodach, here Tiglath-Pileser offered sacrifices to Merodach, and then went on warring against new tribes and gathering fresh prisoners and spoil. A region called Mugan, not otherwise known, was conquered, and after laying these regions under tribute, Tiglath-Pileser returned to Assyria.

In the year B.C. 736 the attention of Tiglath-Pileser was again called to the affairs of Ararat. Sarduri king of Ararat, although checked by his defeat at the hands of Tiglath-Pileser in B.C. 743 still exercised considerable power, he made raids into the neighbouring territory, and raised inscriptions at his capital Turuspa, (modern Van) claiming to have plundered Assyria and Babylonia. Tiglath-Pileser first attacked and conquered the region at the foot of Mount Naal, which lay between his territory and Armenia, this region was easily overrun

G

and added to the boundary of Assyria, and to secure his
future operations, the Assyrian monarch built a city in
Ulluba called Assur-basa, and placed a military governor
in it.

All these preparations being completed, in b.c. 735
Tiglath-Pileser crossed the frontier and invaded Ararat.
Sarduri retreated to his capital Turuspa, on the borders
of Lake Van, and Tiglath-Pileser followed him and
besieged him there. The city of Turuspa was too
strong to be taken by assault, so the Assyrian monarch
setting up a monument of his conquests outside the
city, proceeded to ravage the country for an extent of
seventy kaspu, or about 450 miles, meeting with no
opposition anywhere, the inhabitants confining themselves to their fortresses, and not venturing out against
the invaders. Scarcely had Tiglath-Pileser returned
from this raid when he was summoned in a new
direction.

Azariah the warlike king of Judah whom Tiglath-
Pileser had defeated in his former Syrian war, had died,
and Jotham his son reigned in his stead. Menahem,
the king of Israel, who had given tribute to Tiglath-
Pileser, had died, and his son and successor Pekahiah
had been murdered by Pekah, who had usurped his
throne. Just before the death of Jotham king of
Judah, Pekah king of Israel, and Rezon king of
Damascus agreed to attack Judah, and to place a king
of their own on the throne instead of Ahaz son of
Jotham. Just at this time Jotham died, and Ahaz, who
was a prince of weak mind, and only twenty years old,
mounted the throne of Judah. The united armies of
Syria and Israel invaded Judah, and carried captive

hosts of the people. The army of Israel is stated to have slain 120,000 men in one day, and to have carried off 200,000 women and children to Samaria.

Taking advantage of the trouble of Judah, the Philistines had attacked the south of the country, and captured many cities, while the Edomites defeated the Jews and carried many into captivity. In his extremity Ahaz sent an embassy to Tiglath-Pileser and submitting to him asked his aid against his enemies.

Tiglath-Pileser had known the late king of Judah as warlike and independent, and no doubt it was gratifying to his pride to see the successor of his old enemy forced to submit to him and ask his aid. His own influence in Palestine had never extended beyond Samaria, but the submission of the king of Judah enabled him now to push his empire as far as Egypt.

Under these circumstances, Tiglath-Pileser readily accepted the submission of Ahaz, and in B.C. 734 set his army in motion towards Syria. Rezon king of Syria, and the various princes who with him had attacked Judah, now threw off the Assyrian yoke and prepared to meet the Assyrians. Marching towards the territory of Damascus, Tiglath-Pileser first engaged the forces of Rezon king of Syria, which he found drawn out in battle array against him. Tiglath-Pileser inflicted on the army of Rezon a total defeat, the charioteers of the Syrian army were captured and the chariots broken, the horses, soldiers, the various corps of the army, the archers and men bearing shields, and the spearmen of Rezon, were taken prisoners and the army totally broken up. Rezon fled alone like a deer from the battle-field to save his life, and entered the great gate of his capital city Damascus, trusting to the strength of its fortifications to protect him. This decisive battle and the total overthrow of Rezon, laid the way open for the conquest of Palestine, and struck terror into the hearts of the smaller princes who had relied on the power of Rezon. Tiglath-Pileser now led his army to Damascus, after crucifying the captains of the Syrian army who had fallen into his hand, and closely invested the Syrian capital.

Tiglath-Pileser tells us that he shut up Rezon in Damascus like a caged bird, and cut down all the fine forests round the city for use in the siege, not leaving a single tree near the capital. Several places round were spoiled, and sixteen districts of Damascus were destroyed like a flood. The city of Samalla was captured, and 700 people with many oxen and sheep were carried off, 750 women were carried from Kuruzza, many from Irma, and 550 from Mituna ; 591 cities were captured and spoiled, and the whole of the kingdom of Rezon subdued. Damascus however held out, and could only be reduced by famine, so leaving part of his army before the city, Tiglath-Pileser marched against the other rebels. As a rule, among these there was now no open resistance ; after the disastrous defeat of Rezon they confined themselves as much as possible to their cities and fortresses, and waited in fear the coming of the conqueror.

The first to be attacked was Israel, and descending on this country, the Assyrians overran the north of the country and the tribes beyond the Jordan, carrying these into captivity. The cities round Samaria and the places on the west of the Jordan were also attacked, and all but Samaria captured. Samaria for the present escaped, and there Pekah king of Israel took refuge, while his country was plundered and reduced to a desert.

The kings of the Ammonites and Moabites, whose territories lay on the east of Jordan, had not hitherto been subject to Assyria, but they had joined Rezon in his attack on Judah and in his resistance to the Assyrian power, Tiglath-Pileser now overran their countries and punished them, placing them under tribute.

Passing down out of Samaria, the Assyrian monarch next attacked the Philistines, hitherto independent of Assyria ; Ekron and Ashdod were conquered, Mitinti of Askelon had been active in the war against Judah, and had relied on the power of Rezon to shield him against the Assyrians ; on hearing of the total over-throw. of the army of Damascus, and the siege of Rezon in his capital, Mitinti was overcome with fear, and laid hands on his own life to escape the vengeance of Tiglath-Pileser. Rukupti his son, who then ascended the throne, submitted to Tiglath-Pileser.

Hanun king of Gaza trusted to his proximity to Egypt for protection, but Tiglath-Pileser sent a force against Gaza, and. Hanun fled into Egypt. After this the Assyrians plundered and occupied Gaza, and seeing no help from Egypt, Hanun returned and sub-mitted to Tiglath-Pileser, who restored him to his throne but placed upon him a heavy tribute.

Passing now to the East, the Assyrian army sub-dued the land of Edom, the place of the bitterest enemies of the Jews, and Tiglath-Pileser then attacked

Samsi queen of the Arabs. Zabibe, the former queen of Arabia, had been subject to Assyria, and when Tiglath-Pileser recognised the accession of Samsi, the Arabian queen had sworn by the sun, the great deity of Arabia, to be faithful to Assyria, but afterwards she had revolted and joined the league headed by Rezon. Samsi was defeated and the Assyrians fell upon the various Arab tribes, carrying captive vast numbers of people, with 30,000

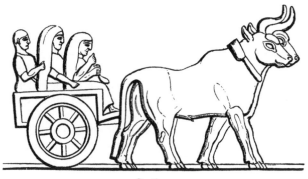

Captives.

camels and over 20,000 oxen. Samsi is said to have fled like a wild ass of the desert, but she did not long escape, she was captured and brought a prisoner to Tiglath-Pileser, who appointed a governor to watch over her, and restored her to her kingdom. At this time the Sabeans, Idibihilites, and numerous other tribes were subdued, and an Arab chief was appointed to a government in the north of Egypt, that country being then in a disturbed state, and some of the inhabitants having sent an embassy to Tiglath-Pileser.

During all this period the siege of Damascus still went on, and continued through B.C. 733, the city being taken B.C. 732.

The fall of Damascus was the crowning triumph of the war, and Tiglath-Pileser on entering the city, slew Rezon the king, and carried the inhabitants into captivity. In the city of Damascus after the capture, Tiglath-Pileser held a great court, to which Ahaz king of Judah went. The list (f subject monarchs who attended and gave tribute, includes Kustaspi of Kummuha, Urikki of Qua, Sibitti-bahali of Gubal, Envil of Hamath, Panammu of Samalla, Tarhulara of Gauguma, Sulumal of Milid, Vassurmi of Tabal, Ushitti of Tuna, Urpalla of Tuhana, Tuhammu of Istunda, Matabahil of Arvad, Sanipu of Bit-ammana (Ammon), Salamanu (Solomon) of Moab, Mitinti of Askelon, Yahuhazi (Ahaz) of Judah, Qavus-malka of Edom, and Hanun of Gaza.

Although the name of Vassurmi king of Tabal occurs in this list among the subject monarchs, we are told immediately afterwards that he revolted and refused to come to the presence of Tiglath-Pileser.

For this rebellion, Tiglath-Pileser despatched an army against him under the care of one of his generals, who conquered Tabal and deposed Vassurmi, placing on the vacant throne a man named Hulli. Tabal was now laid under a tribute of ten talents of gold, 100 talents of silver, and 2000 horses.

Another of the princes who resisted Tiglath-Pileser was Metenna or Matgenus of Tyre. The Assyrian monarch sent a rabshakeh or high general against Tyre, and that city also submitted. Tyre was at that time the greatest maritime city in the world, and its enormous wealth is shown by the heavy contribution the Assyrian general extracted from it, which included 150 talents of gold, about three tons English weight, the value of which in English money would be about £400,000.

The closing scene of the wars of Tiglath-Pileser in Syria took place in Israel. Pekah king of Samaria was murdered by Hoshea son of Elah, who usurped his throne, and sent and purchased his own recognition as king of Israel, by giving a large present to the Assyrian monarch; Tiglath-Pileser then claims to have placed Hoshea on the throne. The exact date of the murder of Pekah and accession of Hoshea is uncertain, but it took place after the return of Tiglath-Pileser to Nineveh, in the interval from B.C. 731 to 729.

After he had settled the affairs of Syria, Babylonia engaged the attention of Tiglath-Pileser, that country, part of which he had annexed in B.C. 745, had since been distracted by numerous factions, and in B.C. 731 the Assyrian monarch again invaded the country with a view to its conquest.

Marching down to Babylon, Tiglath-Pileser proclaimed himself king of Babylon and king of Sumir and Akkad, offering magnificent sacrifices on the national altars.

Several of the Chaldean chiefs resisted this and were attacked by Tiglath-Pileser. Nabu-usabsi, a descendant of a chief named Silani, ruling at Sarrapanu, was taken and impaled in front of the great gate of his capital. Kinziru of Sape, a descendant of Amukkan, was besieged in his city Sape, many smaller chiefs were slain, cities plundered and people carried into captivity, and Tiglath-Pileser firmly seated himself on the Babylonian throne. While he was besieging Sape, the capital of Kinziru, an embassy came from Maruduk-balidin, the Merodach-Baladan of the Bible, who then ruled at a place called Bit-yakin on the Euphrates near the Persian Gulf.

In the year B.C. 730, for the first time in the reign of Tiglath-Pileser, there was peace; by his wars on every side he had overcome all opposition, and had raised Assyria again to a position of undisputed supremacy.

During next year, B.C. 729, Tiglath-Pileser was engaged in celebrating some great festivals to Bel, the supreme god of Babylonia, and again he performed the same ceremonies in B.C. 728.

While these festivals were in progress a revolt broke out, and in B.C. 727, Tiglath-Pileser started on his last expedition.

The mutilation of the Assyrian annals has lost to us the details of this war, even the name of the country is gone and we only know that immediately afterwards Tiglath-Pileser died, and was succeeded on the throne of Assyria by Shalmaneser IV.

Tiglath-Pileser raised two palaces during his reign; one at Nineveh, on the east side of the palace mound near the bend of the river Khozr, and another, which was finished late in his reign, at Calah, in the centre of the palace mound.

A review of the history of the reign of Tiglath-
Pileser, shows that he was one of the greatest sovereigns who held the sceptre of Assur. Coming to
the throne in a time of national depression, when
strong hostile powers had grown up around Assyria,
within sixteen years he had restored the boundaries
of Assyria, and extended its empire over new regions,
wider than those of any former power, his conquests
extending from East to West, from Persia to Egypt,
over about 1200 miles, and from the Persian Gulf
and part of Arabia in the South to Armenia in the
North, over about 800 miles.

Considerable changes were made in the empire
during the reign of Tiglath-Pileser; he first used to
any great extent the plan of transporting large sec-
tions of hostile populations to other countries, and
of mixing the various races under his sway.

In the time of Tiglath-Pileser kings were deposed
and governors appointed over more distant provinces, and as the limits of the empire were greatly
increased the frontier governors were made generals,
and empowered to conduct military expeditions on
their borders, the king himself now only going to
the more important scenes of operations.

During the reign of Tiglath-Pileser, large numbers
of Syrians and people of Palestine were transported
to Assyria, and the Phoenician or old Jewish
alphabet and language began to be much used in
commercial affairs; Assyrian weights and contract
documents after this period, have often inscriptions
in Phoenician as well as Assyrian.

Shalmaneser IV, king of Assyria, who succeeded

Tiglath-Pileser, has left scarcely any memorials. Nothing is known of his relationship to Tiglath-Pileser, or of his title to the throne, and for some time after his accession in B.C. 727 we have no military expedition, but in B.C. 725, finding that several nations in Palestine had thrown off the yoke of Assyria, Shalmaneser marched there and attacked Tyre and Samaria, which submitted and gave their accustomed tribute. Scarcely however was the back of Shalmaneser turned, when both kingdoms again revolted, being encouraged by Sibahe king of Egypt, the So of the Bible.

In the year B.C. 724 Shalmaneser again invaded Palestine, and marching against Luli (Eluleus) king of Tyre, invested that city. Now many of the Phoenician cities, led on by Sidon, and Accho, and Paloetyrus, revolted against Luli king of Tyre and submitted to Shalmaneser, who with their aid raised a navy to attack the Tyrians from the side next the sea. The Assyrian fleet of sixty vessels and 800 men was afterwards defeated and destroyed by a Tyrian fleet of only twelve vessels, and now Shalmaneser was forced to confine himself to blockading Tyre on the land side. At the time his army was blockading Tyre, Shalmaneser attacked also Hoshea king of Israel, and coming up through the land he besieged Samaria.

The sieges of Tyre and Samaria continued through B.C. 723, and were still in progress in B.C. 722, when Shalmaneser died after a short reign of five years.

It is supposed that the Assyrians were impatient of his long operations in Palestine and his want of

success, and that a military revolution took place in
Assyria, which placed the crown on the head of an
officer named Sargon.

Of the character and work of Shalmaneser little is
known, most of his inscriptions are on trade or
private documents, and these show some attention
to commercial affairs. The majority of the standard
Assyrian weights in the British Museum belong to
his reign. The campaigns of Shalmaneser appear
to have been principally in Palestine, there is however mention in one inscription of an expedition to
Deri, in Babylonia, but no new countries were added
to Assyria, and at his death the influence and power
of the empire were somewhat reduced. Shalmaneser
was devoted to the worship of Nergal, the god of
war, and dedicated some fine ivory furniture to his
temple at Tarbizi, north of Nineveh.

Some scholars have supposed that the warning
given to the Israelites in Hosea x. 14, where they
are reminded of the fate of Beth-arbel, "All thy
fortresses shall be spoiled, as Shalman spoiled Beth-
arbel in the day of battle," refers to the domestic
strife in Assyria at the close of the reign of Shalmaneser, but this is doubtful.

CHAPTER IX.

SARGON, B.C. 722 to 705.

SARGON, king of Assyria, claimed descent from an ancient conqueror, Bel-bani, king of Assyria, but it is probable that this had little to do with his elevation to the throne. He was named after an old Babylonian monarch of great renown, who was worshipped as a demigod.

Sargon was advanced in life when he ascended the throne in B.C. 722, and he held the crown for seventeen years, until his death on the eleventh day of the month Ab, B.C. 705.

As soon as he ascended the throne, Sargon prosecuted the Syrian war with vigour, he kept up the siege of Tyre and stormed the city of Samaria, subduing the whole country of Israel. He then carried away Israel into captivity, 27,200 people being transported from the city of Samaria. The kingdom of Samaria was put an end to, and the rest of the Israelites were placed under an Assyrian governor. We learn from the Bible that the captive people of Israel were spread over the northern provinces of the Assyrian empire and in the cities of the Medes.

During the confusion at the death of Shalmaneser,
Merodach-Baladan, the Chaldean, resolved to seize
on Babylonia, which had now been some years subject to Assyria, and making an alliance with Humba-
nigas king of Elam, he with his assistance conquered
Babylon B.C. 722, while Sargon was engaged in Palestine.

The position of Sargon was now one of some
difficulty, Egypt was stirring up disaffection in Palestine, Ursa king of Ararat was endeavouring to
unite a league against Assyria in the North, and
Merodach-Baladan and Humba-nigas were united
against him in the south.

Turning first to the south, Sargon encountered
the forces of Humba-nigas, who had crossed the
Assyrian frontier to Duran. Here a battle was
fought, B.C. 721, and the Elamite driven across the
border into his own country. Sargon then marched
southward, and ravaged some of the tribes who were
in alliance with Merodach-Baladan, carrying the
Babylonians captive to Palestine.

After this Palestine again claimed his attention.
A man named Ilu-bihid, not related to the royal
family of Hamath, seated himself on the throne of
that kingdom, and proposing to deliver the country
from the Assyrians, led the cities of Arpad, Simirra,
Damascus, and Samaria, into revolt, and Sibahe of
Egypt promising his support, the whole of Palestine
threw off the Assyrian yoke.

On the advance of Sargon with a powerful army,
B.C. 720, Ilu-bihid threw himself into the city of
Gargar (Aroer), where he was besieged and captured

by the Assyrians, and Sargon cruelly flayed him alive. The city was committed to the flames and the rest of the revolters heavily punished. Hamath was colonized by 4300 Assyrians and placed under an Assyrian governor. Passing to the south Sargon punished the Israelites and invaded Judah, here he found that a force had collected against him under the leadership of Hanun king of Gaza and Sibahe of Egypt. The Philistine and Egyptian armies had joined at Raphia, on the road to Egypt, and there awaited the attack of Sargon. At the battle of Raphia, Sargon defeated the allies, and taking the city burned it with fire. Many captives fell into the hands of the Assyrians, including Hanun king of Gaza, who was carried to Assyria.

In his third year, B.C. 719, Sargon was called to the east. Iranzu king of Minni was faithful to Assyria, and paid tribute to Sargon, but his people were warlike and impatient of this submission. Two of his cities, Suandahul and Zurzukka, now threw off his yoke, and in alliance with Mitatti, king of Zikarti, endeavoured to establish their independence. Sargon marched an army into Minni and destroyed the two cities, and carried the people into slavery. About the same time the cities of Zukka, Bala, and Abitikna, sent and made alliance with Urza, king of Armenia, and they also threw off the Assyrian yoke, but these isolated revolts were premature and easily crushed by the Assyrians. Sargon transported the rebellious people to Syria and Phoenicia.

In his fourth year, B.C. 718, Sargon marched against Kakki, king of Sinuhta, who had refused his accustomed tribute.

Sargon swore by the Assyrian gods that he would
punish him, and attacking Sinuhta captured the city
and took Kakki, his wife, his sons and daughters,
his courtiers, and his army, leading them captive to
Assyria.

Sargon now rewarded the neighbouring prince
Matti of Atuna, who was faithful to Assyria, by be-
stowing upon him the province which Kakki had
forfeited by rebellion.

Sargon in his Chariot.

Next year, B.C. 717, Sargon had a more formidable
rebellion to deal with. Pisiri of Karchemesh had
been a faithful subject of Assyria during all the
reign of Tiglath-Pileser, but now from some un-
explained cause he suddenly became hostile, and
sending a messenger to Mita, king of Muski, whose
territories lay on the Black Sea, he made an alliance
with him against Sargon.

Karchemesh, the capital of Pisiri, was a great cen-

96

99

tre of trade and one of the richest places in that
region, and it had enjoyed a long period of peace
and prosperity. Mita, king of Muski, was a new
personage on the stage of Assyrian history, and he
was a determined foe of Assyria. Sargon marched
first against Karchemesh, reserving Mita for another
expedition; he easily captured the Hittite capital and
took an immense spoil. Pisiri, all his family, and
his officers, with gold, silver, and other metals in
great quantities, furniture and ornaments, fell into
the hands of Sargon. The Assyrian monarch placed
in the treasury at Calah eleven talents, thirty manas
of gold, and 2100 talents of silver from the plunder
of Karchemesh.

The people of Karchemesh were led captive and
scattered over the Assyrian empire, while Assyrian
colonists were brought to people the city in their
place, and Karchemesh was formally annexed to Assyria and placed under an Assyrian governor.

The people of the two cities of Papa and La-
lukna, relying on the country of Kakmi, had also
revolted against Assyria, now Sargon sent and punished them, carrying them captive to Damascus.

In the year B.C. 716, the sixth of his reign, Sargon
had to meet the most formidable opposition to his
rule. All the countries along the north and east
of Assyria joined in a confederacy against him,
urged by the two old enemies of Assyria, Ursa of
Ararat and Mita of Muski. Iranzu of Minni was
faithful to Assyria, but his people had already shown
themselves restless under the dominion of Sargon in
B.C. 719. Since that Iranzu had died, and Aza his

son had succeeded to his throne. He still carried
out the policy of his father and remained in submission to Assyria, although his people were ripe
for revolt.

At this time Ursa of Ararat sent messengers to
the districts of Udis, Zikarta, Misianda, and other
parts of Minni, and stirred up the people to revolt
against Assyria. The efforts of Ursa were successful,
and the whole of Minni revolted; they attacked and
murdered Aza their king, and threw his body with
great indignities over a cliff. At the same time
Sargon had arrayed against him Muski, Tubal, Milid,
Atuna, Kar-alla, Allabra, and many other kingdoms.
Sargon immediately led a force into Minni, and
capturing Bagdatti the leader of the rebellion, flayed
him alive over the spot where he had murdered
Aza, and overrunning the whole of Minni, he placed
on the throne Ullusunu the brother of Aza the late
king.

After the departure of the Assyrians, Ullusunu
sent and made alliance with Ursa of Ararat, and
with him joined Assur-liha of Kar-alla, and Itti of
Allabra. These three princes submitted to Ursa,
and agreed to accept his dominion instead of that
of Sargon, but the Assyrian king was again quickly
on the spot, and capturing Izirtu the capital of
Minni, burned the city with fire, the cities of Zibia
and Armaid shared the same fate. Ullusunu and
his family had fled for safety to the mountains, but
now came forward and made a hasty submission,
imploring the mercy of the conqueror. Sargon for-
gave Ullusunu and restored him to his throne, and

then proceeded against the other revolters. Assur-liha of Kar-alla was captured by Sargon and flayed alive, while Itti of Allabra, who also fell into his hands, was transported with his family to Syria. Niri-sar, prefect of Surgadi was captured, and his cities added to the government of Persia. Bel-shazzar, governor of Kisesim, was conquered and carried captive, the name of his city was changed to Kar-masmasu, and an Assyrian was appointed governor.

Kibaba of Harhar had sent and submitted to Dalta of Illiba, but Sargon attacked and captured Harhar, changing its name to Kar-sargon and pla-cing a military governor over it. After this eight chiefs of the Medes gave tribute to Sargon, who had now broken the neck of the revolt in the east of his dominions. The failure for the present of this formidable rebellion, was partly due to the fact that the various parties did not act in concert, but allowed themselves to be taken in detail by the Assyrians, and partly to the inactivity of Ursa, king of Ararat, who after fomenting the rebellion, delayed sending any assistance to the revolters.

In the next year, B.C. 715, the revolt broke out again with great fury. Ullusunu, king of Minni, again threw off the Assyrian yoke and to ensure the aid of Ursa of Ararat, ceded to him a portion of his territory containing twenty-two cities. Ullu-sunu also pressed Dejoices, a powerful governor in Minni, to join him, and sent his son as hostage to him.

Sargon again by his rapid movements disconcerted

the confederates. He marched into Minni and seized the district which Ullusunu had promised to Ursa, and capturing Dejoices, transported him to Hamath. He then overran all the smaller places which were likely to aid in the revolt, and confined the rebellion to the district of Minni.

Sargon then turned his attention to the west, where for some time rebellion had been in progress. Mita of Muski, the leader of the western opposition to Sargon, had slain the king of Que and annexed his territory, Sargon defeated him and recovered part of this territory, which he placed under an Assyrian general, who kept in check the forces of Mita of Muski, Ambaris of Tubal, and other enemies of Assyria in this direction. The next movement of Sargon was to Arabia, where he conquered the Thamudites and several other tribes, carrying them captive and placing them in the cities of Samaria. The power of Sargon was now firmly established, and the rulers near Palestine were anxious to gain his friendship, so while he was in Palestine, Pharaoh king of Egypt, Samsi queen of Arabia, and Ithamar the Sabean, sent him rich presents.

In his eighth year, B.C. 714, Sargon proceeded to Minni, and stamped out the remains of the rebellion. The kings of Minni and Illipa submitted and gave tribute, and Sargon marched against Mitatti of Zikarta ; his troops were easily defeated, and three cities with twenty-four smaller towns were captured, including the capital city, Parda. Mitatti, who had been an active enemy of Assyria all through, fled away from his country. Ursa of Ararat had been inactive while Sargon crushed his allies, and now his turn was to

come. Sargon attacked him with fury, destroying his
army and capturing 260 of the royal tribe of Armenia.
Ursa himself fled, and escaped by the swiftness of his
mare from the battle-field, and took refuge in his
mountain fastnesses. A considerable part of his territory was now ravaged, and some districts which the
Armenians had wrested from Minni, were restored to
that country. Yanzu king of Nahiri, in his capital
Hupuskia, now paid his accustomed tribute of horses,
oxen, and sheep.

Sargon now resolved to strike a blow at the power
of Ararat. South of the country lay a rugged mountainous district, the capital of which was Muzazir, a large
city posted on a rocky eminence, and strongly fortified.
Here was the great shrine of the god Haldi, the
supreme god of the people of Ararat and other northern
nations; and the temple was rich with the offerings of
many kings, and with statues of the great rulers of
Ararat, who venerated the deity Haldi, and his companion, or consort, Bagmasti. Sargon prepared an
expedition and marched against Muzazir, penetrated
the mountains, and appeared before the city. Urzana
king of Muzazir, on seeing the approach of the Assyrian
army, would not trust himself to his capital, but fled
into the mountains, leaving the defence of his capital
to his army. Sargon then attacked and stormed the
city, and committed it to the flames. The city was
plundered, its temple rifled, and its gods, wealth, and
people, carried off. The wife, sons, and daughters of
Urzana, with all his treasures, thirty-two talents, eighteen manas of gold, 160 talents, two and a half manas
of silver, 20,000 people, 692 mules, and immense
numbers of oxen, sheep, asses, and other animals, were

carried off, the images of the gods Haldi and Bagmasti,
and the offerings dedicated in the temples, and stores
of rich dresses, were also brought to Assyria. The
district of Muzazir was annexed to Assyria, and a
military governor placed over it.

Ursa king of Ararat on hearing of the disaster and
the captivity of his god Haldi, was overcome with
grief, and committed suicide, running himself through
with his sword. Over all the country of Ararat there
was now lamentation at the loss of their god and
death of their monarch.

Secure now on his northern frontier, Sargon turned
his attention to the east, where revolt was again breaking out. He marched, B.C. 713, into the region of
Illipa, Media, and Kar-alla. After Sargon had killed
Assur-liha of Kar-alla, the people of that region had
raised up Amidassi his brother, who continued the
opposition against Sargon. On the approach of the
Assyrian army to Kar-alla, Amidassi and his principal
followers fled, and Sargon pursued them, and overran
a considerable portion of Illipa and Media. Most of
the kings and chiefs in the east now submitted, including Ullusuna of Minni, Dalta of Illipa-bal-idina of
Allabra, and forty-five chiefs of the Medes, among
these are several well-known names, including that of
Arbaku or Arbaces.

The next operations of Sargon were against the
western confederacy, which had so long opposed him,
and he selected Tubal for his first attack. Vassarmi
king of Tubal had been deposed by Tiglath-Pileser,
and a man named Hulli raised to the throne in his
place. Hulli, although he owed his elevation to the
Assyrians, revolted against Shalmaneser king of Assyria,

and was by that monarch deposed, and carried captive to Assyria.

Sargon when he ascended the throne befriended Hulli, and restored him to the throne which he had lost by rebellion; and on the death of Hulli soon after, the Assyrian monarch confirmed Ambaris his son in the kingdom of his father, gave him his own daughter in marriage, and bestowed upon him the neighbouring country of Cilicia as a dowry.

Ambaris, like his father, was guilty of great ingratitude, and when Ursa of Ararat, and Mita of Muski, raised the great rebellion against Assyria, Ambaris joined them. The king of Tubal from that time made incursions into the Assyrian empire, and led Matti of Atuna and other princes into revolt. For some years Sargon had been unable to take any steps against Ambaris, but now that he had conquered most of the other revolters, he marched against him.

He attacked and conquered the country of Tubal, sending Ambaris into slavery, and placed the country under an Assyrian governor.

In his tenth year Sargon attacked Tarhunazi, king of Milid, who had conquered and taken possession of the district of Kummani, and was in rebellion against Assyria.

Sargon marched against him, and overran the whole of Kummani, then attacking the city of Milid the capital of Tarhunazi, he captured and destroyed it, carrying away an immense spoil. Tarhunazi fled from Milid to the fortress of Tul-garimmi, where he was taken by the Assyrian monarch, together with a considerable portion of his army. Tarhunazi was placed in irons, and with his wife, sons, and daughters, and five thousand of his people, transported to Assyria. Sargon then restored the town of Tulgarimmi, and made it the capital of a district, over which he placed one of his generals as governor.

In this region Sargon now took possession of some other cities which controlled the roads leading into Muski, as Mita king of Muski was always hostile to Assyria.

In this year Sargon was gathering materials for the building of Dur-Sargina (Khorsabad), and he collected cedar and other woods from the Lebanon region. Among the other places which supplied to him material for this work, he mentions Bahal-zabuna (Baalzephon) and Ammon.

In his eleventh year, B.C. 711, Sargon marched to Syria against Gauguma. Tarhulara, king of Gaugama, had been for some years a faithful ally of Assyria, recently he had been murdered by his son Muttallu, who had placed himself on his father's throne, and revolted against Assyria. Muttallu was captured with his family and adherents by Sargon, who placed Marqasi the capital under an Assyrian governor.

After conquering Gaugama Sargon marched into Palestine, where all the south of the country was in revolt. Azuri the former king of Ashdod had stirred up revolt against Assyria, and had made alliances with the kings around against Sargon. For this Sargon had deposed him, and had given his crown to his brother Ahimiti; but the people of Ashdod were dissatisfied with the new ruler, and they revolted against him, and set up a man named Yavan, whose recommendation was his hostility against Assyria. Yavan now set to work to raise a confederacy against

Assyria, and led the Philistines to revolt, and joined with Judah then ruled by Hezekiah, Moab, and Edom. All these sent an embassy to Pharaoh king of Egypt and asked his aid against Assyria. Pharaoh held out encouragements to the revolters, but did not give them any assistance when the hour of danger came. Sargon learning of the revolt came to Palestine, and Egypt failing to help, Yavan fled on the approach of Sargon, crossed the boundary of Egypt, and ultimately delivered himself up to the king of Meroe or Ethiopia. With the flight of Yavan the rebellion collapsed, and the cities of Ashdod and Gimtu (Gimzo) were taken by Sargon. The king of Meroe, anxious to be on friendly terms with Assyria, took Yavan, and bound him, and sent him in chains to Sargon.

This expedition of Sargon is mentioned in chaps. xviii–xx of Isaiah, where there is a remarkable condemnation of the conduct of Egypt. The whole of the first thirty-nine chapters of Isaiah are full of allusions to the political events of this period of Assyrian history, and Isaiah's remarks on the bad faith and impotence of Egypt, are fully borne out by the relations in the Assyrian inscriptions.

In his twelfth year, B.C. 710, Sargon attacked Merodach-Baladan, the Chaldean, the prince who sent an embassy to Hezekiah.

Eleven years had now passed since Sargon made his former attack upon Merodach-Baladan, and that period had been spent in incessant conflict, resulting in the reconquest and the consolidation of the empire. Being now at peace on all sides, Sargon determined on the conquest of Babylonia.

Merodach-Baladan aware of his expedition, looked

to Elam for aid. Humba-nigas the king of Elam, who had helped him on the former occasion, was now dead and Sutur-nanhundi or Sutrak-nanhundi, reigned in his stead, and to him Merodach-Baladan sent for help. Sargon advanced along the east of the river Tigris and first attacked Dur-athara, a city situated on the river Surappi. This city was fortified and difficult of approach, as the Chaldeans had flooded the country round the town, by piercing the banks of the river. Dur-athara was taken by the Assyrians, and they then proceeded to subdue the region on the east of the Tigris, watered by the two rivers Surappi and Ukni. Many chiefs and cities were conquered, while Merodach-Baladan made no movement to help them.

Sargon then turned to the east, and entered the Elamite territory at the province of Yatbur, and stormed the cities of Samhana and Bab-dur, then crossing into Rasi, he attacked and captured Bit-imbi, driving before him Sutrak-nanhundi king of Elam, who retired to the mountains.

The object of Sargon in this diversion appears to have been to check the Elamite monarch, and prevent him coming to the aid of Merodach-Baladan. The Babylonian prince had gathered his treasures and sent them as a present to Sutrak-nanhundi, imploring his aid, but after Sargon had ravaged Rasi and Yatbur, the Elamite king would not bring his army to face the Assyrians.

Sargon now marched to the Euphrates, and crossing to the western side, entered Dur-ladinna, a town belonging to the Dakkuri, a tribe of Chaldeans near Babylon. On the approach of Sargon, Merodach-Baladan would not risk a battle to save his capital, but abandoned Babylon and retreated to Ikbi-bel. Babylon was now entered in triumph by Sargon, who declared the reign of Merodach-Baladan an usurpation, and proclaimed himself king of the country. He then celebrated the sacred rites performed by the monarchs, and promoted public works.

Next year, B.C. 709, Sargon started from Babylon against Merodach-Baladan, who had retreated from Ikbi-bel to his castle of Bit-yakin. Merodach-Baladan had strengthened his wall, and excavated a new moat outside the city, 200 cubits (330 feet) wide, and one-and-a-half gar (thirty feet) deep ; then piercing the embankment of the Euphrates, he had led the waters by a canal into his moat, and throwing bridges across the waters, had passed his army in. Sargon contrived to cross the water with his troops, and then caught the followers of Merodach-Baladan as in a net;—a great slaughter took place, and Bit-yakin with all its treasures fell into the hands of Sargon. Merodach-Baladan and his family were captured, and the whole country as far as the Persian Gulf, acknowledged the sway of the Assyrian monarch.

B.C. 708. While Sargon stayed at Babylon, the governor he had appointed at Que conquered Mita king of Muski, and in the same year Uperi king of Dilmun, on the Persian Gulf submitted, and seven of the kings of Cyprus in the Mediterranean also gave tribute. Sargon sent over to Cyprus a stelé of himself, which was discovered in the island, and is now in the Berlin Museum. Muttallu king of Kummuha, who had revolted against Assyria, and trusted to Argisti king of Ararat, but when the Assyrians advanced against him, Argisti did not help him, and he fled and left his country, which was reduced to the condition of an Assyrian province, and peopled by the prisoners from Bit-yakin.

In the year B.C. 707 Sargon was again involved in a war with Elam. Dalta king of Illipa had died, and his two nephews, Nibe and Ispabara, disputed about the succession to the throne, and raising their partizans commenced a civil war. Nibe sought and obtained the aid of Sutrak-nanhundi king of Elam, and with his help took possession of the capital Marubisti. Ispabara then sought the aid of Sargon, who in his fifteenth year sent seven generals and their troops to help him. These defeated the Elamites at Marubisti, and placed Ispabara on the throne as tributary of Sargon. The Elamites now began a desultory war along the frontier, and Sargon being too old and infirm to march against them, they captured the districts of Hahiri and Raza, about B.C. 706.

Soon after this Sargon died, and was succeeded by his son Sennacherib, on the twelfth day of the month Ab, B.C. 705.

Sargon rebuilt the temple of Nebo and Merodach at Nineveh, and repaired part of the palace of Assur-nazir-pal at Calah; but his greatest work was the building of the city of Dur-sargina (now Khorsabad), a city about ten miles from Nineveh. Dur-sargina is one of the most perfect specimens of Assyrian towns.

The walls of Dur-sargina formed a square over one mile each way, and on the north-west face stood the palace platform, in the shape of the letter T, on the outer and northern portion of this platform, Sargon built his palace, the halls and chambers of which were panelled with slabs of alabaster, richly adorned with sculptures, and inscribed with the titles, exploits, and annals of the reign of the monarch.

In all the royal inscriptions and historical texts of Assyria, while long details are given of the wars and buildings of the kings, nothing is said about the state of the people, but from the reign of Sargon downwards we gain from numerous contracts, leases, letters, and other private documents, a better knowledge of the state of the country, and the manners and customs of its people.

Looking at the history of the reign of Sargon, it appears that the Assyrian empire consisted of a central portion of territory incorporated with Assyria, outside this a fringe or border of tributary states, and beyond this a series of independent powers, the greatest of which were Egypt on the south-west, Armenia or Ararat on the north, and Elam on the south-east. These larger powers, fearful that they in turn might be attacked by the Assyrians, endeavoured to weaken the power of the empire by stirring up revolt among the tributaries near them. The conduct of the Egyptians towards the Jews during the Assyrian period forms a good type of the action of the other independent powers they encouraged to revolt, and when the hour of danger came withheld their aid, or sent help that was worse than useless.

Sargon king of Assyria was a ruler of great talent, but he was engaged all his reign rather in consolidating the empire than in extending it. The principal new nations that appear on the stage in his time are the people of Cyprus, the Muski or Moschi on the Black Sea, and the state of Dilmun on the Persian Gulf.

CHAPTER X.

SENNACHERIB, a younger son of Sargon, succeeded
his father on the throne of Assyria, on the twelfth day
of the month Abu, in the eponymy of Pahir-bil, prefect
of Amida, that is, according to our reckoning, about
the sixteenth of July, B.C. 705, and was assassinated
about the month Debitu, in the eponymy of Nabu-ahi-
eris prefect of Samalla (December, B.C. 681), having
reigned about twenty-four years and five months.
Soon after he ascended the throne he found himself
involved in a formidable war with Babylonia. On the
death of Sargon another of his sons was made king at
Babylon, but after a brief reign he died, and the
Babylonians raised in his place a man named Hagisa.
Hagisa after a reign of one month was murdered by
Merodach-Baladan, who once more seated himself on
the Babylonian throne. The new triumph of Merodach-
Baladan was short, for his forces and those of his ally,
the king of Elam, were defeated three months later by
Sennacherib at the battle of Kisu, and he was again a
fugitive, B.C. 704. After the usual course of devastation,
Sennacherib set on the throne of Babylon a native of

the country named Bel-ibni, who had been brought up
in the palace of Sargon king of Assyria. On the
crowning of Bel-ibni, B.C. 703, Sennacherib returned in
triumph to Nineveh, carrying with him crowds of
captives, and heavily laden with the spoil of the conquered region.

After having settled the affairs of Babylonia, Sennacherib turned his attention to the east of his dominions,
to the region of the Yasubigalla and Kassi. These
peoples inhabited the mountainous region between
Assyria and Persia, north of Elam. They were a
warlike and independent race, and had not yet been
subjected to the Assyrian yoke. The nature of the
country was rugged and mountainous, covered with
forests and without roads. The usual course of chariot
riding was generally impossible, and in his invasion
Sennacherib rode on horseback, and sometimes even
went on foot.

Marching into the country the Assyrians attacked
the three cities of Bit-kilam-zah, Hardispa, and Bit-
kubatti. These places, which were fortified, they
captured, together with many villages round them, and
carried off numbers of people, horses, mules, asses,
oxen and sheep. Numbers of the tribes who dwelt in
tents were plundered and their encampments destroyed,
and to secure the permanent subjugation of the district, Sennacherib rebuilt Bit-kilam-zah, and fortified it,
placing there an Assyrian garrison.

Most of the inhabitants of the district had retreated
to the mountains on the advance of Sennacherib, but
he now persuaded them to return, and to re-enter the
cities of Hardispa and Bit-kubatti, and he placed the

whole district under the care of the governor of
Arapha. After setting up a memorial of his victories,
Sennacherib turned against the country of Elippi, near
the modern Ispahan. Izpabara, who had been placed
on the throne by Sargon, had not kept the Assyrian
alliance, now on the approach of Sennacherib he fled,
and the Assyrian army swept the land of Ellipi like a
storm. The capital Marubisti, and the city of Akkuddu,
together with thirty-four other towns, were captured
and burned, and the wealth of the people carried off.
A district of Ellipi, comprising the cities of Zizirtu,
Kummahu, and Bit-barra, was added to Assyria, and
placed under the prefect of Harhar. The city of
Ellinzas was rebuilt and fortified to hold these conquests, and it was named the city of Karu-Senna-
cherib.

While in Ellipi some of the tribes of the Medes,
hearing of the warlike vigour of Sennacherib, sent him
presents to propitiate his favour, and made submission
to Assyria.

This eastern expedition of Sennacherib occupied
the year B.C. 702, and at the close of this year, his
southern and eastern borders being secure, he had
leisure to turn his attention to the affairs of Palestine.

Encouraged by the king of Egypt, Hezekiah king
of Judah had thrown off the Assyrian yoke, several
of the smaller sovereigns had either voluntarily joined
him or been forced to submit to the king of Judah,
and Lulia (the Elulius of Josephus) king of Tyre and
Zidon, had also rebelled against Sennacherib. The
Assyrians had lost their hold on all the country
from Lebanon to Arabia, and Sennacherib resolved to

reconquer this region.   Crossing from his capital into
Syria, which he calls the land of the Hittites, he attacked first Lulia king of Zidon; but this prince was
not prepared to resist Sennacherib, so he embarked
on one of his vessels from the city of Tyre, and set
sail for the land of Yatnan (the island of Cyprus),
abandoning his country to the mercy of the Assyrians.
Sennacherib now besieged and took the various Phoenician towns; Tyre the strong city appears to have
successfully resisted him, but he captured Zidunnu-
rabu (great Zidon, Joshua xix. 28) and the lesser
Zidon, then coming south Bit-zitte and Zariptu
(Zarephath, 1 Kings xvii. 9), Mahalliba Usu (Hosah,
Joshua xix. 29), Akzibi (Achzib, Joshua xix. 29), and
Akku (Accho, Judges i. 31).   The sea coast of Phoenicia, down to the land of the Philistines, was now in
the hands of Sennacherib, and he raised a man named
Tubahal to the throne of Zidon, and fixed upon the
country an annual tribute.

The success of Sennacherib along the coast, and
the failure of Egyptian aid, now brought nearly the
whole of Palestine to his feet, and the various rulers
sent envoys with tribute, and tokens of submission to
present before the Assyrian monarch.   Menahem
who ruled at Samaria, Tubahal the newly made
king of Zidon, Abdilihiti king of Arvad, Urumelek
king of Gebal, Metinti king of Ashdod, and Buduil
king of the Ammonites, Kemosh-natbi king of the
Moabites, and Airammu king of Edom, now made
their peace, and Askelon, Ekron, and Judah alone
remained in rebellion.   Sennacherib started from
Akku, and keeping along the coast, invaded Askelon,

and capturing Zidqa the revolting king, sent him, his wife, his sons and daughters, his brothers and other relatives, captive to Assyria.

The cities of Askelon, Bit-daganna (Beth-dagon, Joshua xv. 41), Yappu (Joppa, Jonah i. 3), Benai-barqa (Bene-berak, Joshua xix. 45), and Azuru, were successively captured, and Sennacherib placed Saru-ludari the son of Rukibti, on the throne. Moving from Askelon Sennacherib attacked Ekron: he tells us that Padi king of Ekron had been faithful to his pledges to Assyria, and the priests, princes, and people of Ekron had conspired against him and revolted, and putting their king in bonds had delivered him into the hands of Hezekiah king of Judah, to be kept prisoner at Jerusalem. The revolters at Ekron relied on the assistance of Egypt, and when Sennacherib advanced against the city a force under the king of Egypt came to their assistance. The Egyptian army was from the kings of Egypt (the plural being used), and from the king of Miruhha or Ethiopia. To meet the army of Egypt, Sennacherib turned aside to Altaqu (Eltekeh, Joshua xix. 44), where the two forces met, and the Egyptians were defeated. The over-throw of the Egyptian army was followed by the capture of Altaqu and Tamna (Timnah, Joshua xv. 10), and Sennacherib again marched to Ekron, and put to death the leading men of the city who had led the revolt, and severely treated the people. Their king, Padi, was demanded of Hezekiah king of Judah, and being delivered up was once more seated on his throne. The last part of the expedition given in the Assyrian annals, consists of the attack on Hezekiah.

The king of Judah was the most important of the tributaries who had thrown off the yoke of Assyria, and was reserved for the last operations. After settling the affairs of Ekron, Sennacherib marched against Judah, and captured forty-six of the fortified cities of Hezekiah, agreeing with the statement of the Book of Kings, that he came up against all the fenced cities of Judah and took them ; all the smaller places round them were destroyed, and Sennacherib carried into captivity 200,150 people of all sorts, together with horses, mules, asses, camels, oxen, and sheep, in great numbers. Sennacherib goes on to relate that he shut up Hezekiah in Jerusalem like a caged bird, and built towers round the city to attack it. Sennacherib now began to portion off and dispose of the territory which he had conquered. The towns along the western side he detached from Judah, and divided them between Metinti king of Ashdod, Saru-ludari king of Askelon, Padi king of Ekron, and Zilli-bel king of Gaza, the four kings of the Philistines who were now in submission to Assyria, and he increased the amount of the tribute due from these principalities. Hezekiah and his principal men, shut up in Jerusalem, now began to fear, and resolved on submission. Meanwhile the soldiers of Sennacherib were attacking Lacish, one of the last remaining strong cities of Judah. The pavilion of this proudest of the Assyrian kings was pitched within sight of the city, and the monarch sat on a magnificent throne while the Assyrian army assaulted the city. Lacish, the strong city, was captured, and from thence Sennacherib dictated terms to the humbled king of Judah. Hezekiah sent by his messenger and made submission, and gave tribute, including 30 talents of gold, 800 talents of silver, precious stones of various sorts, couches and thrones of ivory, skins and horns of buffaloes, girls and eunuchs, male and female musicians. According to the record of Sennacherib he returned to Nineveh in triumph, bearing with him this tribute and spoil, and not a single shadow of reverse or disaster appears in the whole narrative.

The accounts of this expedition of Sennacherib, given in the Bible, relate that after the submission of Hezekiah, "the angel of the Lord" went through the camp of the Assyrians, and destroyed 185,000 men of Sennacherib's army, and that the Assyrian monarch returned in disgrace to Nineveh. This overthrow of Sennacherib's army is confirmed by a story told to Herodotus by the Egyptian priests. They relate that in the time of an Egyptian king named Sethos, Sennacherib made an expedition against Egypt, and came as far as Pelusium. Sethos went out against him with an inferior army, having invoked the aid of the Egyptian gods, and been promised deliverance. In the night, as the two armies lay opposite each other, hosts of field-mice came and destroyed the bowstrings of the Assyrians, who next morning fled.

Such is a brief outline of the story, which is in singular agreement with the statement of the Bible; we cannot however expect to find any direct confirmation of the overthrow of Sennacherib from the Assyrian inscriptions, as it was not the custom of these ancient nations to record their own defeats.

Excepting this single circumstance, the agreement, between the Assyrian and Biblical records is very close, the principal difference being that in the annals of Sennacherib the events are given at greater length.

In the year B.C. 700 Sennacherib marched southward a second time to Babylonia. After the conquest of Babylonia, B.C. 704, Merodach-Baladan had hidden in the marshes near the Persian Gulf, and as the Assyrian generals kept up a search for him he abandoned the country, and taking on board his boats the images of his gods, he set sail for Nagitu, an Elamite city on the Persian Gulf, with a view of founding a colony there, out of the reach of the Assyrian power.

After the emigration of Merodach-Baladan and his followers, a Chaldean chief named Suzub, son of Gahul, took the lead in the opposition to Assyria, and collected a force at the town of Bit-tutu in the lake region. Suzub became so formidable that Sennacherib himself marched against him and routed his forces at the city of Bit-tutu. Suzub fled from the battle, and hid himself like his predecessor.

Sennacherib now spoiled the whole region of Bit-yakin and southern Babylonia, and at the close of the expedition set up his eldest son, Assur-nadin-sum, as king at Babylon. Thirty thousand soldiers, captured in this expedition, were distributed over the empire and incorporated in the Assyrian army.

The fifth expedition of Sennacherib took place somewhere about the years B.C. 699–698, and it was directed against the rugged region laying north-west of Assyria. From the region of Lake Van, north of Assyria, a mountain chain runs along from east to

west, terminating in Asia Minor; in its western part
now called the Taurus, but the whole of it in Assyrian
times called mount Nipur. The tribes attacked by
Sennacherib in his fifth expedition lived in the highlands round this mountain chain, and west of the
Euphrates, having on the south Cilicia, and on the
north Tubal and Moski.

These hardy races inhabited the cities of Tumurra,
Sarum, Ezama, Kipsu, Halbuda, Qua, and Qana,
places situated on the rocks and mountains like nests
of eagles. In his campaign in this region Sennacherib and his soldiers encountered great hardships, and
in some places had literally to climb the rocks after
the enemy. All these difficulties were, however, overcome, and the district conquered by the Assyrians.
Sennacherib then attacked Maniyahe, king of the
Dahe, whose capital was the city of Ukku, and captured the city, Maniyahe taking to flight on the
approach of the Assyrians. Next Sennacherib overran part of the forests of Cilicia, and wound up by
destroying the city of Tul-garimmi, which was on the
borders of Tubal.

The sixth expedition of Sennacherib embraces a
series of operations carried on for three or four years
against the Chaldeans.

About B.C. 997 Sennacherib determined to crush
the tribe of Chaldeans who had emigrated from Babylonia and settled in Elam, but instead of trying to
force a passage through the hostile country of Elam,
he resolved to fit out a naval expedition and attack
them from the Persian Gulf. For this purpose he
made two establishments for shipbuilding, one at Tel-

barsip or Kar-shalmaneser on the Euphrates, and the other at Nineveh on the Tigris; here he collected Phoenician and Syrian workmen, and fitted out a considerable fleet. To man the vessels he engaged sailors from the Ionians, Tyrians, Zidonians, and other maritime peoples on the Mediterranean. The vessels were then floated down the Euphrates and Tigris, until they were in water deep enough to allow of their being laden with the troops and stores, after which the expedition proceeded down the river to the mouth of the Euphrates. Here, at the place where the waters of the river mingle with the ocean, Sennacherib performed sacrifices to Hea, the god of the sea, and with grand ceremonies rode out into the ocean and dropped into the water images of ships and fishes made of gold, as offerings to the deity, to obtain his blessing on the expedition. The region where the emigrant Babylonians had settled was situated at the mouth of the Ulai or Eulaeus river, and embraced the cities Nagitu, Nagiti-dihiban, Hilman, Billatu, and Huppanu. The rapid accumulation of alluvial deposits has, however, now removed the sea some miles from the scene of these events, which probably took place near the modern city of Mohammerah. Sailing along the coast, the fleet of Sennacherib came in sight of the mouth of the Eulaeus and the cities of the Chaldeans. The emigrants and their Susian allies, aware of the projected invasion, had collected a large force, and now lined the shore to await the landing of Sennacherib, who successfully disembarked his troops and attacked and defeated the Chaldeans. All the new settlements were then plundered, and the fleet of Sennacherib sailed back laden with the spoils.

On the return of the expedition Sennacherib found
that a new revolt had broken out at Babylon; Suzub,
the Chaldean, whom he had defeated, had returned,
and receiving assistance from the king of Elam, had
proclaimed himself king; the Babylonians who had
emigrated to Elam, finding no peace or security there,
and Merodach-Baladan, their old leader being dead,
had returned to their own country, and swelled the
party of Suzub, who was conducted to Babylon by the
king of Elam, and installed in the government there.

The generals of Sennacherib were at once on the
alert, and marching against Suzub, defeated his forces
and captured him.   Suzub was sent bound to Sennacherib at Nineveh.   The Assyrian army then fell
upon the city of Ereck, and sacked it, carrying away
its gods, and then turning against the king of Elam,
fought a battle with him, in which Sennacherib claims
the victory.

The source of all the trouble experienced by Sennacherib in Babylonia was the neighbouring state of
Elam.   The Elamites inhabited a considerable stretch
of country on the east of the Tigris, partly plain near
the river, the rest mountainous towards Persia.

The Elamites were a restless warlike people, always
interfering in the affairs of Babylonia, and generally
hostile to Assyria.   Sennacherib now resolved to
punish them for this, and to recover a strip of territory
which they had wrested from Assyria in the time of
Sargon.

The Assyrian monarch first attacked and recovered
the cities formerly belonging to Assyria, and placed
them under the control of the governor of Duran,

then crossing the frontier into Elam he captured the
cities of Bube, Dunni-samas, Bit-risiya, Bit-ahlami,
Dur, Dantesula, Siliptu, and many others, in all thirty-
four strong cities, and numerous villages round them;
the whole of these were set on fire, and the Assyrian
monarch tells us that the smoke of their burning like
a vast cloud concealed the face of the heavens.
Kudur-nanhundi the Elamite heard of the capture of
his cities, but had not the courage to go out and meet
Sennacherib, his only efforts were to fortify some of
his remaining cities, he did not dare even to stay in
his capital, Madaktu, but hastily retreated to the royal
city of Haidala, situated in the mountains, and far
from the scene of hostilities.

It was now December when Sennacherib gave
orders to advance against Madaktu, the Elamite
capital, but the winter set in with unusual intensity
and saved the city. Rain and snow fell in heavy
showers, filling the streams and making the roads im-
passable, and Sennacherib reluctantly turned and gave
up the attempt.

Kudur-nanhundi king of Elam did not live three
months after this campaign; he died suddenly, and
was succeeded by his brother Umman-minan, a prince
of a totally different disposition.

After these events, somewhere about B.C. 692, the
Babylonians meditated revolt, and began to rebuild
the walls of their city. Suzub had escaped from
captivity, and made his way back to Chaldea, where
he once more raised the standard of rebellion, when
being surrounded by the troops of Sennacherib he
eluded pursuit and fled to Elam, where he received for

a time an asylum. In Elam a considerable body of
followers, fugitives and others, gathered round him,
and he now came at the head of these followers to
Babylon. His party within the city admitted him,
and he once more ascended the throne. Suzub, foreseeing that he would soon be attacked by Sennacherib,
and aware that he could not resist the Assyrians without aid, broke open the treasuries of the temple of Bel
at Babylon, that of Nebo at Borsippa, and of Nergal
at Cutha, and sent the gold and silver as a present to
Umman-minan, king of Elam, with the following
message: " Gather thy people, prepare thy camp, to
Babylon come and strengthen our hands, for a master
of war art thou."

Umman-minan, burning to revenge the destruction
wrought by Sennacherib in his last campaign, readily
accepted the offer of Suzub, and collected a numerous
body of auxiliaries to go to Babylon. His army contained Persians, Elamites, people of Anzan, Ellipi, and
other Median tribes, Chaldeans, and others from the
coast, with Nabu-zikir-iskun, son of Merodach-Baladan,
Sennacherib's old enemy, together a numerous gathering, and at the head of these Umman-minan arrived
at Babylon, and joined the forces of Suzub; Umman-
minan and Suzub took up their position at the town
of Halule by the side of the Tigris, and there awaited
the attack of Sennacherib. The Assyrian monarch
describes in vivid and poetical language the appearance of this vast and motley host, and relates his own
preparations to attack.

The battle ended in the total rout of the Babylonian
and Elamite armies; their leaders were slain or taken

prisoners, their charioteers were killed, and horses with empty chariots were galloping in confusion over the field; the dead crowded the battle-field, and the war horses and chariot of Sennacherib waded through pools of blood and rode over heaps of slain. Suzub king of Babylon, and Umman-minan king of Elam saw the overthrow of their forces from their royal pavilion in the middle of the army, and mounting their chariots endeavoured to ride through the fugitives, but afterwards, abandoning their carriages, they dismounted and fled on foot from the fatal field. After the close of the battle commenced the spoiling of the dead; the golden ornaments of the chiefs, and the ornamented arms which they had worn in expectation of triumph the day before, were now laid at the feet of Sennacherib, and he sent a detachment of chariots after the fugitives, who rode down and destroyed many who had escaped from the field. The battle of Halule ended operations for the year, but next spring, about B.C. 691, Sennacherib marched into the country again to complete his work. Suzub was no longer able to bring a force into the field, but he had done what he could to fortify Babylon, and resolved to stand a siege. Sennacherib appeared before the city, his army prepared with every means of attack, and he proceeded regularly to invest the place, which he soon afterwards successfully stormed. Babylon was now wholly given up to an infuriated soldiery, its walls were thrown down, its towers demolished, its people given up to violence and slavery, the temples rifled, and the images of the gods brought out and broken in pieces. The city was given to the flames, and to complete the destruction the Assyrians pierced the embankment of the canal, called the Araxes, and let the waters flood the city. Babylon was now reduced to such a condition that its inhabitants could not again rebel against Sennacherib. Suzub appears to have fallen into the hands of the Assyrians again, but he once more escaped; his time, however, was drawing near, soon after he was thrown from his horse and killed, and with him perished every vestige of resistance to the Assyrian power. Now for ten years Babylonia remained at peace, until the accession of Esarhaddon.

After this Sennacherib made another expedition to Palestine, the details of which are most of them lost. It was probably at this time, about B.C. 690, that Sennacherib defeated the Greek fleet off the Cilician coast and founded the city of Tarsus. Further south he again overran Palestine, and penetrating into Arabia, stormed the city of Edom, and carried off the spoil and gods of the king of Arabia, several of the Arabian tribes were ravaged at this time, and their spoil carried to Assyria.

Some writers have supposed that two expeditions against Palestine are mentioned in the account 2 Kings xviii, in the first Sennacherib being successful, while in the second his army was overthrown. Certainly Sennacherib gives us no sign of disaster to his first expedition to Palestine, and the supposition of two expeditions would account for the fact; but at present our information is not sufficient to decide the question, as from the mutilation of Sennacherib's records, we do not know whether he attacked Judah in his second Syrian expedition or not.

There is one thing which speaks in favour of Sennacherib's overthrow being at the later date, B.C. 690. After his first expedition, B.C. 701, the Assyrian army was strong enough on its return to attack Babylon next year, B.C. 700, but after the second expedition to Palestine, B.C. 690, the warlike expeditions cease, and no more campaigns are recorded, while the Elamites ravaged the southern border of Assyria without check, which they would hardly have dared to do when Sennacherib was powerful. During the last nine years of his reign Sennacherib dwelt at Nineveh, where he built a palace for his son, Assur-munik or Assur-mulik, probably the Adrammelek of the Book of Kings, who was heir to the throne after the death of his eldest son, Assur-nadin-sum, B.C. 694.

Towards the close of the year B.C. 681, Adrammelek and Sharezer, two sons of Sennacherib, conspired against their father and murdered the monarch while he was worshipping in one of his temples, after which they endeavoured to grasp the crown.

When Sennacherib ascended the throne he built a palace at the city of Kalzu, but soon abandoning this, he commenced to pull down and rebuild the palace at Nineveh, which he ultimately made the grandest royal residence in Assyria. This palace, which he finished about B.C. 695, was about 1500 feet long and 700 feet broad, it contained three great courts and numerous halls and chambers, panelled with carved and inscribed slabs of alabaster, showing the magnificence and power of the king, and the high state of cultivation of the arts.

After he had finished this palace, Sennacherib

restored the palace on the mound of Nebbi-yunas, and built the wall round the city of Nineveh, a gigantic fortification eight miles in circumference.

The captives taken in the king's various wars, people of Palestine, Cilicians, Medes, Babylonians and others, were forced to toil on these vast public works; they raised the earth for the mounds, made the bricks for the walls, and dragged intó their places those vast colossal figures which adorned the porches and doors of his buildings.

Sennacherib may be taken as the typical eastern monarch: all the vices of pride and arrogance, cruelty and lust of power, so conspicuous in Oriental sovereigns were developed to excess in him; he had not the genius of his father Sargon, who resembled Darius Hystaspes in his character and reign, but Sennacherib was more like the Persian monarch Xerxes; his military expeditions were on a grand scale, but more designed for show than real conquest; his greatest efforts sometimes bore no fruit or only ended in disaster; he had no genius for conciliating the peoples he conquered, and his process for putting an end to revolt is shown by the ruin he inflicted on Babylon.

The character of Sennacherib is vividly and truthfully pourtrayed in those magnificent passages in the Books of Kings and Isaiah, where his messages to Hezekiah king of Judah are related; his proud and violent reign had a fitting termination in a violent death at the hands of his own sons.

CHAPTER XI.

ESARHADDON, B.C. 681 TO 668.

ESARHADDON was a younger son of Sennacherib, and appears to have been absent from Nineveh at the time when his brothers Adrammelek and Sharezer murdered their father, and he resolved to contest the empire with them. Both sides gathered large armies, and they came to a decisive battle in the land of Hani-rabbat near the upper Euphrates. Here Esarhaddon defeated the army of his brothers, and Adrammelek and Sharezer fled from the field into the land of Armenia and received shelter there, the king of Armenia being hostile to Assyria.

After the battle, January B.C. 680, Esarhaddon entered Nineveh in triumph, and in a few days started for the south to settle the affairs of Babylonia, then disturbed through the action of the sons of Merodach-Baladan. Nabu-zir-napisti-esir, a son of Merodach-Baladan, ruled his father's original dominions by the Persian Gulf, and now declared himself independent, and raising an army went up to attack the city of Ur (Muqheir), which was then governed by a prince named Ningal-idina. Ur fell into the hands of the

Chaldean prince, who aspired to the government of
Babylonia. The Assyrian generals were ordered to
proceed against him, and Nabu-zir-napisti-esir retreated
before the forces sent against him by Esarhaddon and
fled across the frontier into Elam. The Chaldean
prince and his brother Nahid-maraduk appealed for
protection to Umman-aldas king of Elam, but the
Elamite refused him shelter, and anxious to be on
friendly terms with Esarhaddon, put Nabu-zir-napisti-
esir to death.

Nahid-maraduk, seeing the death of his brother, felt
that Elam was not a safe place and preferred to
implore the mercy of Esarhaddon, so he hastily re-
crossed the frontier and threw himself at the feet of
the Assyrian monarch, who not only pardoned him
but restored to him the dominions of his brother on
the sea coast.

Arriving at Babylon Esarhaddon commenced the
restoration of that city, which had been much damaged
by the wars in the time of Sennacherib his father
and had remained almost a ruin since its capture in
B.C. 691. Esarhaddon rebuilt the walls and raised
again the temple of Bel, and he brought back from
Assyria the various images of the gods which Sennacherib his father had carried captive to Assyria,
and restored to the Babylonians the plunder of their
cities. He thus conciliated the people, and proclaiming
himself king of Babylon as well as Assyria, passed
much of his time in his southern capital.

During the latter part of the reign of Sennacherib,
while Babylon was under a cloud, the chief of the
Dakkuri, the tribe of Chaldeans on the edge of the

desert west of the city, Samas-ibni by name, had plundered the lands belonging to the inhabitants of Babylon. Esarhaddon took Samas-ibni and burned him, restoring the fields to the people of Babylon and Borsippa, and he raised up Nabu-salim son of Balasu to be king of the Dakkuri. Bel-basa king of the Gambuli, a tribe inhabiting the marshes near the Persian Gulf, submitted himself to Esarhaddon and was favourably received by the Assyrian monarch, who assisted him to fortify his capital city Sapi-bel under agreement that he should hold it against the Elamites who were generally hostile to Assyria.

The affairs of Babylonia being settled, Esarhaddon turned his attention to Syria; there Abdi-milkutti king of the commercial city of Zidon, who ruled Phoenicia, had made alliance with Sandarri king of Sisu and Kundi, and they had sworn together by the names of the great gods to revolt against Assyria. Esarhaddon marched against Zidon and besieged the city, which he captured and destroyed. Abdi-milkutti and Sandarri fell into the hands of Esarhaddon, who beheaded them and sent their heads as trophies to Nineveh. Esarhaddon, in order to complete the ruin of Zidon, built a new town near it, which he peopled with the captives from the other city and placed under the control of an Assyrian general; his effort was evidently to divert the trade of Zidon to his new settlement, but the commerce lost at the destruction of Zidon flowed to the sister city of Tyre.

At this time the whole of Palestine and the surrounding places submitted to Esarhaddon, who gives us a list of the kings, twelve belonging to the mainland and ten to Cyprus; these are Bahal king of Tyre,

K

Manasseh king of Judah, Qavus-gabri king of Edom, Musuri king of Moab, Zilli-bel king of Gaza, Mitinti king of Askelon, Ikasamsu king of Ekron, Milki-asapa king of Gebal, Matan-bahal king of Arvad, Abi-bahal king of Samaria, Budu-il king of Beth-ammon, Ahi-milki king of Ashdod, all belonging to the coast and Palestine; and Aegistus king of Idalium, Pithagoras king of Kidrusi, Kin-.... king of Soli, Ithuander king of Paphos, Erisu king of Salamis, Damastes king of Curium, Karmes king of Tamissus, Damos king of Ammochosta, Unasagus king of Lidini, Puzus king of Aphrodisia, ten kings of the island of Cyprus.

All these monarchs sent presents, and Esarhaddon directed them to supply him with building materials for the palace he was building at Nineveh.

Esarhaddon now began to turn his attention to Egypt, and although he did not at once attack it he took the city of Arza, which was situated on the small stream called the river of Egypt, dividing that country from Palestine.

In the time of Esarhaddon commenced the migration of the wandering tribes across the Caucasus. The Cimmerians who lived in this region were now coming south and gradually occupying Asia Minor and Armenia. A branch of these nomads proceeded as far south as the land of Hupuskia on the east of Assyria, led by a chief named Teuspa. Esarhaddon determined to check these inroads and marched to Hupuskia, where he defeated the Cimmerians and killed their leader; the Cimmerians checked in the south then turned to the west and overran part of Asia Minor.

The hardy mountaineers of Cilicia and Duhua or Dahe had thrown off the Assyrian yoke after the expedition of Sennacherib, and now required a further lesson to force them to submit to the Assyrian dominion. Esarhaddon invaded this region, and spreading fire and sword over their country compelled them once more to submit to the Assyrian yoke.

The next expedition of Esarhaddon was to the district of Eden which the Assyrians called Tel-assar [1], which lay in the mountains south-east of Assyria, it was subdued again by Esarhaddon.

Esarhaddon then attacked the Medes; the Manni or Minni were attacked; they were allies of Ispakai king of Asguza, and in the war Ispakai was killed, but the Minni do not appear to have suffered, and afterwards continually made inroads into Assyrian territory. In Media further districts were subdued, Patusarra near Bikni being the extent of the conquests in this direction. Two of the chiefs of this region, Sidirparna and Eparna, were brought prisoners to Nineveh, and Uppis lord of Partakka, Zanasana of Pardukka, and Ramatea of Urakazaparna, three Median chiefs, came in person to Nineveh to submit to Esarhaddon.

Esarhaddon now determined on a greater and much more difficult enterprise, the conquest of Arabia. The arid and difficult nature of the Arabian territory, and the want of means of access to it, had prevented any serious attempts to conquer the country. For nearly two hundred years the Assyrians had come in contact with outlying tribes on the borders of Syria and the Euphrates, and Tiglath-Pileser, Sargon, and Sennacherib, had all made some conquests near Edom, but none of them had penetrated far into the country. The circumstance which turned the mind of the Assyrian

---

[1] Isaiah xxxvii. 12.

K 2

king in this direction appears to have been this. Sennacherib his father having carried off the gods of the kingdom of Edom in Arabia, Hazail king of that district made a journey from Arabia to Nineveh to supplicate Esarhaddon for the return of these gods, and agreed to pay a heavy tribute in return. Esarhaddon, having carved an inscription on the idols in honour of his deity Assur, restored them to Hazail, who departed from Nineveh an Assyrian tributary. After this Esarhaddon determined to conduct an expedition into Arabia and subdue the country. In this campaign he relates that he travelled a distance of 140 kaspu, or about 900 miles; he reached two districts, named Hazu and Bazu. probably the Uz and Buz of the Bible, and assailed and defeated eight kings and queens who reigned in these parts; these were Kisu king of Haldile, Akbar king of Napiatu, Mansaku king of Marabanu, Yapah queen of Dihtan (Dedan), Habisu king of Kadesh, Niharu king of Gahpanu, Bahilu queen of Idilu, Habanamru king of Budah. Esarhaddon declares that he swept their followers like a field of corn and carried away their gods, their goods, and their people to Assyria.

After the return of Esarhaddon to Nineveh, Laile king of the city of Yedih, a ruler from these parts who had fled when his country was invaded by Esarhaddon, sent an embassy to Nineveh to ask for the return of the images of his gods which the Assyrian army had carried off, and he made submission to Esarhaddon and brought presents to the monarch.

Esarhaddon granted the petition and restored the gods, and invested Laile with the title of king of Bazu or Buz.

Other events, which happened in the Arabian penin-
sula, also served to increase the influence of Esarhaddon. Hazail, who had first submitted to Esarhaddon,
died, and his son, whose name is variously written
Yahlu, Yahta, Yautah and Vaitah, sent to Esarhaddon
and received from that monarch confirmation of his
title to the throne, and paid to the Assyrian king an
additional tribute of ten manas of gold, fifty camels,
precious stones, and other things. Some of the
Arabian tribes were dissatisfied with Yahta, and a
chief named Wabu set himself up against him. The
revolt became so formidable that Yahta was compelled
to invoke the aid of Esarhaddon, who sent an army to
Arabia and defeated the insurgent tribes. Wabu was
captured by the Assyrians and carried captive to
Nineveh.

Esarhaddon now determined to diminish the danger
to the Assyrian empire on the west by conquering
Egypt, a country which for two hundred years had
been a thorn in the side of the Assyrians. Egyptian
influence had been at the bottom of most of the
opposition and revolts in Palestine, and although the
Egyptians seldom supported the rebels with a military
force, their proximity to Palestine and their hostility
to Assyria caused constant trouble to the Ninevite
monarchs.

In the latter part of the eighth century B.C. the
Egyptian monarchy had broken up and the country
had come under the influence of the Ethiopians.
Sabaku the Ethiopian had conquered Egypt, and had
died leaving his crown to a monarch named Sabatok
after whom came Tirhakah the brother-in-law of

Sabaku. Tirhakah at first ruled in Upper Egypt and Ethiopia, and afterwards drove out the various kings who ruled in Lower Egypt and united the whole country under one sceptre. Tirhakah had been the enemy of Sennacherib, Esarhaddon's father, and it was his army which opposed Sennacherib at the time of the disaster to the Assyrian host, since this Tirhakah had claimed to have conquered the Assyrians and had persuaded the king of Tyre to throw off the Assyrian yoke. Bahal king of Tyre had increased in power and riches since the destruction of Zidon, and while he was subject to Assyria Esarhaddon had showered favours upon him. Esarhaddon had entered into a convention with Bahal by which, in return for services rendered by the Tyrians, the Assyrian monarch ceded to the king of Tyre a considerable portion of the coast of Palestine including Accho[1], Dor[2], and all the northern coast of the Philistines with the cities, and Gebal[3], and Lebanon, and the cities in the mountains behind Tyre.

Tyre was now in the height of its prosperity, and Bahal, feeling strong enough to become independent, entered into the designs of Tirhakah king of Egypt, and relying upon that monarch revolted against Assyria. It is probable that the alliance between Tirhakah and Bahal carried the rest of Palestine into revolt and closed the Mediterranean to the Assyrians. This serious defection in the western provinces brought Esarhaddon again into the field; he came up against Tyre and instituted a strict blockade, but there was no chance of reducing the city while her fleet had command of the Mediterranean and Egypt was in alliance with her; Esarhaddon therefore resolved to effect the

---

[1] Judges i. 31.   [2] Joshua xii. 23.   [3] Ezekiel xxvii. 9.

conquest of Egypt, and starting from Aphek in the north of Palestine he marched along the coast road to Raphia on the borders of Egypt. Here he suffered much for want of water, and was assisted in his difficulty by the king of Arabia. Crossing the frontier of Egypt Esarhaddon met and routed the army of Tirhakah, and pursued the Ethiopian monarch to Memphis, which city Esarhaddon entered in triumph, Tirhakah making a hasty retreat up the Nile. At Memphis the wife and concubines of Tirhakah, his relatives, his officers, and the images of his gods, gold, silver, precious stones, valuable articles of clothing, furniture and stores, fell into the hands of Esarhaddon. Memphis was at this time the capital of Egypt, and its possession ensured the country to Esarhaddon, who now journeyed up the Nile to Thebes the capital of Upper Egypt, which he made the limit of his empire.

Esarhaddon now divided the whole of Egypt from Thebes to the Mediterranean into twenty governments, and placed the majority of these under native Egyptian princes, who submitted to his rule, but a few important posts he garrisoned by Assyrian troops and placed under Assyrian governors.

The following is a list of these governments and their rulers: Necho king of Sais and Memphis, Saruludari king of Zihanu (Sin or Pelusium), Pisan-hor king of Natho, Paqruru king of Pisabtu, Pukkunanni-hapi king of Athribis, Nahke king of Henens, Petubastes king of Zoan (Tanis), Unammon king of Natho, Harsieses king of Zabnut, Buaima king of Mendes, Sheshonk king of Busiris, Tafnacht king of Bunubu, Pukkunanni-hapi king of Ahni (Heracleopolis), Ipti-hardesu king of Pizatti-hurunpiku, Bukur-ninip king of Pahnuti,

Ziha king of Siyout, Lamintu king of Chemmis, Ispi-
madu king of Tain (Abydos), Manti-mi-anhe king of
Nia (Thebes). Necho, the first king in this list, was
supposed to be the legitimate monarch, and head of
these kings.

Egypt is called in the annals of Esarhaddon by its
scriptural name Muzur, but sometimes also Magan,
an old Turanian name, signifying the ship-region,
Ethiopia is called Cush as in the Bible, but sometimes
also Miruhha or Miluhha (Meroe), the Nile is called
Yaruhu, like the יארה in Exodus i. 22. Esarhaddon
rebuilt several of the cities of Egypt, and called them
by Assyrian names, and fixed a tribute on all the
Egyptian kingdoms.

Beside the campaigns mentioned in his annals,
Esarhaddon carried a number of the Israelites captive,
and replaced them by colonies of Babylonians, and he
bound Manasseh king of Judah and brought him to
Babylon.

Esarhaddon rebuilt the walls of Babylon and the
temple of Bel at that city, he built a palace at Nineveh,
and late in his reign began one at Calah, but died
before it was finished, he also built a palace for his son
Assur-bani-pal at Tarbizi (Sherif Khan), near Nineveh,
and another at Calah. Esarhaddon died after a reign
of thirteen years, B.C. 668, leaving four sons and one
daughter. Esarhaddon was a ruler of considerable
ability, and extended the bounds of the empire, particularly by his conquest of Egypt and Arabia; at his
death, there only remained two powers of importance
outside the pale of the Assyrian empire, Armenia
and Elam, and these were generally at peace with
Assyria during his reign.

CHAPTER XII.

REIGN OF ASSUR-BANI-PAL UNTIL THE CONQUEST OF

KARBAT.

ASSUR-BANI-PAL, the eldest son and successor of Esarhaddon, was the greatest of the Assyrian monarchs; he was known to the Greeks under the name of Sardanapalus, and some have supposed him to be the Arsnappar of the Book of Ezra.

At the time Esarhaddon started for Egypt, Assur-bani-pal began to aspire to the throne, and after the return of his father from his Egyptian expedition, Esarhaddon was impressed with the belief that the Assyrian gods had willed that Assur-bani-pal should be associated with him on the throne, and he in consequence called together a meeting of the people of Assyria, and publicly proclaimed his son king, on the twelfth day of the month Iyyar.

The exact year of this event is not known, but it happened somewhere between B.C. 671 and 668, the date of Esarhaddon's death.

Soon after the commencement of the reign of Assur-bani-pal disastrous news arrived from Egypt. After the return of Esarhaddon to Assyria, Tirhakah, king of Ethiopia, communicated with his partizans in Egypt, and raising a large army had descended once more the banks of the Nile. Thebes had fallen into his hands, and he had advanced and captured the city of Memphis. The kings and governors appointed by Esarhaddon fled before him, he once more made himself king of Egypt, and fixed his capital at Memphis, while the adherents of Assyria were sent into exile.

It was at once determined to send an army to recover Egypt from Tirhakah, and Assur-bani-pal took command and started for Syria. Assur-bani-pal and his army arrived in Syria, and passed along by the coast of the Mediterranean. Here he relates that the twelve kings of Palestine and the ten kings of Cyprus gave the accustomed tribute, and among the names in the list are Tyre and Judah. These lists of tributaries are, however, open to some suspicion, for during the last campaign of Esarhaddon, Tyre was in rebellion against Assyria and besieged by the forces of Esarhaddon, and when we next hear of it it was besieged by Assur-bani-pal and there is no notice of the capture or submission of the city in the interval. It is most probable that the city was besieged the whole time by the Assyrian army, and that the name of the king of Tyre in the tribute list of Assur-bani-pal's first expedition was only written there to flatter the vanity of the Assyrian monarch. After receiving the submission of these kings, Assur-bani-pal marched to Egypt, and crossed the frontier to a city named Kar-banit.

Tirhakah, aware of the advance of the Assyrian army, collected his army and sent it out under the control of a general from Memphis, where he there held his court. The Egyptian general took up his position at Kar-banit, and on the arrival of the army of Assur-bani-pal at that town, the army of Tirhakah was attacked and routed, and the young Assyrian monarch set out to march to Memphis.

News was brought to Tirhakah that his forces were overthrown, and he, abandoning his capital Memphis, took a boat and ascended the Nile to Thebes, leaving Lower Egypt to the conquerors. The rabshakeh, or commander in chief of the Assyrian army, was now joined by the various petty kings who had formerly been the tributaries of Esarhaddon, and who had been expelled from Egypt by Tirhakah. These petty kings brought their forces and a fleet of boats, and the Assyrian generals ascended the Nile with them to expel Tirhakah from Egypt. The journey from Memphis to Thebes occupied the Assyrians and their allies forty days, and when they arrived at Thebes they found Tirhakah had abandoned the place and retreated to Ethiopia, where he now fixed his camp. Assurbani-pal occupied Thebes with his army, and now again proceeded to divide Egypt among the kings who had been appointed by his father, he however placed the country under heavier bonds and stronger garrisons, in the hope of preventing another revolt, but Tirhakah was not pursued into Ethiopia, and all the valley of the Nile above Thebes was left to him, and no provision was made to prevent his attempts to regain the country.

This was a fatal flaw in the arrangement, and as

soon as the Assyrian army had retired Tirhakah
renewed his attempts to regain possession of the
country.

The Egyptian people, now under the sway of
Assur-bani-pal, began to feel the weight of the
Assyrian yoke, and even the kings who owed their
rise to Esarhaddon longed to be rid of the foreign
dominion, and felt that a composition with Tirhakah
was better than the rule of Assur-bani-pal. The
generals of Assur-bani-pal were vigilant, and his forces
so strong that open rebellion was useless, so several
of the kings under the leadership of Necho of
Sais, Saruludari of Pelusium, and Paqruru of Pisabtu,
formed a secret conspiracy, and having taken counsel
together, they sent an embassy to Tirhakah, in
Ethiopia, offering, if he would swear to them that
they should not be disturbed in their principalities,
that they on their part would transfer their allegiance
from the Assyrian monarch to him, and they proposed that he should descend the Nile with an army,
while they at the same time raised a revolt in
Egypt, and that they should join forces with him
and expel the Assyrians.

How far these negotiations had proceeded we do
not know, but before the project could be carried
out, the Assyrian generals suspecting what was
going on, captured a messenger going from the
kings to Tirhakah, and learned the whole plot.
The Assyrian commanders were only just in time,
but they promptly arrested Necho and Saruludari,
and sent them in chains to Assyria; Paqruru escaped,
and some of the Egyptian cities, finding the plot

was discovered, broke into a premature revolt, while Tirhakah resolved to risk the attempt, and invaded Egypt. The cities of Sais, Mendes, and Zoan or Tanis, which had revolted, were taken by the Assyrian generals, their walls thrown down and great slaughter made among the inhabitants, the troops of Assur-bani-pal then marched against Tirhakah, and defeated and drove him once more out of Upper Egypt. Overcome by this last reverse, and feeling his case hopeless against the Assyrians, Tirhakah soon afterwards died.

Meanwhile Necho and Saruludari were carried as prisoners to Nineveh to Assur-bani-pal, but the Assyrian monarch now changed his policy towards Egypt, and tried conciliation instead of rigour. His prisoner Necho, the late king of Memphis and Sais, was the leader of the Egyptian governors, and the representative of the old royal family of Egyp.. Assur-bani-pal pardoned Necho his rebellion, and investing him with royal robes, gave him valuable presents, and Necho having submitted to him again, he sent a new force with him into Egypt, with directions to restore to Necho all his former dominions and to proclaim his son, who received the Assyrian name of Naboshasban, king in Athribis.

The new expedition arrived in Egypt and in the native city of Necho, Sais, proclaimed him once more king, and his son ruler in Athribis.

A new power was however now rising on the scene. Tirhakah, worn out by his contests with Assyria, had died, but his sceptre had passed to younger and more vigorous hands. He was succeeded by

Nud-ammon, the son of Sabaku, a former Egyptian
king, and of the sister of Tirhakah. The new monarch ascended the throne at Napata, the capital of
Ethiopia. Soon after this he had a dream, in which
he saw two serpents, and it was interpreted by the
astrologers to mean that as he now possessed the
south (Ethiopia), he should also conquer the north
(Egypt), after this the king marched to the north
and was welcomed at Thebes, which city he made
his capital and the centre of his operations, he advanced then and took Unu (Hermopolis), which he
also fortified. The people of Lower Egypt had
been restless under the new arrangements made by
Assur-bani-pal and Paqruru was still at large and the
head of the opposition to the Assyrian power. The
Assyrian generals collected their forces against Nud-
ammon, but his success was such that they retired
and shut themselves up in the city of Memphis,
where they were followed by the Ethiopian monarch,
who assaulted and captured the city and put an end
to the Assyrian dominion. Paqruru now came forward as the leader of the Egyptian governors, and
submitted to Nud-ammon.

Assur-bani-pal now heard the news that the Assyrian power was driven out of the valley of the
Nile, and he ordered a new expedition to recover
the lost country.

The second Egyptian expedition of Assur-bani-pal
started for the west; according to one account,
under the direction of the king himself, according to
another text under one of his generals. The army
crossed the frontier of Egypt, and Nud-ammon no

sooner heard that the Assyrian army was in Egypt, than he started from Memphis and fled to Thebes. Memphis now opened its gates to the Assyrians, and the various kings and chiefs came forward and renewed their submission to Assur-bani-pal. From Memphis the Assyrian army started for the south, to punish the city of Thebes. The defection of Thebes to the Ethiopians during the last war, was in a great measure the cause of success of Nud-ammon, and the Assyrian monarch resolved to take vengeance on the city.

On approaching Thebes, the Ethiopian monarch was found to have fled again, this time he ascended the Nile to a place named Kipkip. Through the whole time Nud-ammon had never faced the Assyrian army, and his reverse on this occasion was as signal as his success when he advanced into Egypt.

On entering the city of Thebes the Assyrian army commenced the work of destruction. No city in the world had such a splendid series of public monuments; these temples, statues, obelisks and palaces, the work of ages during the glory of Egypt, were now as far as possible disfigured and destroyed. The Assyrians carried away silver and gold, precious stones, the furniture of the palace, robes of various materials, horses, people, male and female, elephants and monkeys. Two of the great obelisks which stood in front of one of the temples were taken to Nineveh as trophies; they are stated to have weighed 2500 talents or about seventy tons English weight. The Assyrians boast that they swept the city like a flood, and the army returned from Egypt laden with spoil. All the kings, tribute and institutions, which the Assyrians had set up in Egypt before, were now restored but only for a time; for, although, whenever they met in open field, the Assyrians easily defeated the Egyptians, the country was too powerful, and lay too far from Assyria to be permanently held by them. The sacking of Thebes in this war is described by Nahum, ch. iii.

The next efforts of Assur-bani-pal were directed against the city of Tyre. The siege of Tyre had been commenced by Esarhaddon, and the city was probably invested for some years until the third expedition of Assur-bani-pal. The position of Tyre on the sea coast, and its large navy and commerce, rendered it difficult to establish an efficient blockade, as supplies could always come from the sea.

The Assyrians pressed the city in a systematic way, they built towers round it from which they could assail the city, they took possession of and blocked up all the roads, and endeavoured to command the channels into the city, access to all the wells round the city was cut off, and this first reduced the city to a strait. The supply of water within the city was inefficient, and the inhabitants were in time obliged to mix sea water with their drinking water; this could not last long, and the king of Tyre was forced to send out and offer to submit to Assyria. He had revolted in expectation of Egyptian assistance, and continued his resistance as long as there was any hope of help from that quarter, but the ease with which Assur-bani-pal had expelled Nud-ammon from Egypt and the short supply of water in Tyre made him lose all hope of holding out against Assyria. The embassy from the king of Tyre was headed by Yahimelek, his son and heir to the throne, and in addition to the tribute of the country, Assur-bani-pal demanded the daughter of the king of Tyre, and the daughters of his brothers in marriage, with rich dowries, and added these princesses to his harem. Tyre was at this time the greatest commercial city in the world, and its surrender to Assur-bani-pal at once spread his fame over numerous countries which had never been within reach of the Assyrian arms, and the smaller kingdoms on the coast of the Mediterranean now followed the example of Tyre, and submitted to Assyria. First among these came Yakinlu or Ikkilu, king of Arvad a small island on the Mediterranean, which had often given tribute to Assyria before. Assur-bani-pal was already known for his desire to possess a large harem, and Yakinlu sent, together with rich presents, his daughter to the Assyrian monarch.

Some time later Yakinlu died, and his ten sons disputed as to the succession to the crown, they all ultimately resolved to lay their case before Assur-bani-pal and abide his decision. The names of these ten princes show the influence of the worship of Baal among the Phœnicians, eight of them having the name of this god in their proper names. These ten princes were Azibahal, Abibahal, Adonibahal, Sapadibahal, Budibahal, Bahalyashub, Bahalhanun, Bahalmaluk, Abimelek, and Ahimelek. Assur-bani-pal received the princes in state, and chose Azibahal as king of Arvad, sending the others back with rich presents and marks of favour.

Mugalli, king of Tubal, sent to Nineveh his daughter also, and paid a tribute of horses to Assur-bani-pal; and Sandasarmi, king of Cilicia, followed the same example, adding his daughter to the harem of the great Assyrian monarch. The submission of Mugalli and Sandasarmi put an end to the constant border warfare which had gone on for some years in the highlands of Asia Minor.

At this time there existed in the south-west corner of Asia Minor a rising state named Lydia. Herodotus in his history informs us of the murder of Candalus, the king of Lydia, by his officer Gyges, who then married the queen and usurped his late master's throne. Gyges was now ruling over Lydia and although far from the range of Assyrian expeditions, he heard of the glories of the great king of Assyria, the conqueror of Tyre and Egypt, and the Assyrian annals further relate that he had a dream, in which the god Assur, the great god of the Assyrians, appeared to him and commanded him to send an envoy and make submission to Assur-bani-pal.

Soon after this a man in strange dress and with stranger speech came to the frontier of Assyria, and was sent to the capital of Assur-bani-pal as a curiosity, and was brought before the king.

A parade was made of men speaking the various languages from the east and the west, who were under the sway of Assur-bani-pal, but for some time no one could be found with whom the stranger

could communicate. When his errand was interpreted, it turned out that he was the messenger of
Gyges, king of Lydia, who had sent, in obedience to
the vision, to give tokens of submission to the king
of Assyria.

Some time after this Gyges sent a second embassy
to Assur-bani-pal with rich presents, and the am-
bassador related that since Gyges had submitted to
Assyria and had honoured the gods of Nineveh, he
had been successful in war against the Cimmerians,
and he sent by the hand of his envoy two chiefs of
the Cimmerians bound in fetters as a present to the
Assyrian king.

These professions of friendship between the two
sovereigns were however hollow, and when soon
after Psammitichus was at war with Assyria, Gyges
sided with him against Assur-bani-pal.

Psammitichus was son of Necho, king of Memphis
and Sais, and succeeded his father in those districts
of Egypt early in the reign of Assur-bani-pal. Possessed of the greatest share of territory among the
kings of Egypt, and having the capital Memphis
in his dominion, he soon began to aspire to the
government of the whole country, and sent to Gyges
to make an alliance with him against Assyria.
Assur-bani-pal was at the time engaged in wars in
other directions, and Gyges, forgetting all his em-
bassies and promises of submission, sent a force to
assist Psammitichus in conquering the other Egyptian
governors and expelling the Assyrian garrisons from
Egypt. Egypt now finally passed out of the Assyrian empire, and Assur-bani-pal on hearing of the

loss and of the defection of Gyges king of Lydia, lifted up his hands to his gods and invoked a curse on the head of the Lydian sovereign.

At this time the Cimmerians were spreading over the highlands above Assyria; they had been checked by the defeat inflicted upon them by Esarhaddon, and Assur-bani-pal, when crown-prince, had a little later commanded a force against them, they had since turned into Asia Minor and attacked Lydia during the reign of Gyges. After the revolt of Gyges and Psammitichus from Assyria, the Cimmerians again attacked Lydia, perhaps this time prompted by Assur-bani-pal. In a battle with them Gyges lost his life, and these nomads then overran all Lydia except the citadel of Sardes the capital. Some time later Ardys, son of Gyges, who had succeeded to his father's throne, expelled the barbarians, and then sent and renewed the connection between Lydia and Assyria. By his messenger he stated to Assur-bani-pal that all the evils which had happened to Gyges and Lydia had been caused by his father's faithless conduct to Assyria.

The embassy of Ardys to Nineveh occurred late in the reign of Assur-bani-pal, and was a barren solace to the pride of the Assyrian monarch, whose western wars had resulted in the loss of Egypt to the empire.

CHAPTER XIII.

THIS period in the history of Assur-bani-pal probably extended over about twelve years, from B.C. 660
to 648, but Assur-bani-pal has left very little evidence
as to the dates of his various expeditions.

On the south-eastern border of Assyria, near the
frontier of Elam, lay the district of Yamutbal, the
capital of which was Duran or Deri. Duran was
the seat of a governor whose business it was to
watch the Elamites who held the fortress of Bit-imbi,
and a small stream running between this city and
Duran was considered the boundary between the two
countries.

The district of Yamutbal was open on its eastern
side to the attacks of the mountaineers who inhabited the rugged region of the Zagros, and a
band of these, under a chief named Tandai, inhabited
the city of Karbat in the district of Halehazta.
These people, feeling secure in their mountain fortress and the difficult nature of their territory, defied

the Assyrian power and constantly made plundering excursions into the plains of Yamutbal.

The people of Duran, suffering from these incursions, petitioned Assur-bani-pal to check them, and he gave orders for the generals in that neighbourhood to move their troops against Karbat. The Assyrian army advanced and captured the city, taking Tandai alive and carrying off a great spoil.

This expedition to Karbat happened before the revolt of Psammitichus, for the people of Karbat who were conquered were transported by Assur-bani-pal to Egypt.

The next expedition of Assur-bani-pal was against the land of Minni. Minni lay to the south-east of Ararat or Armenia, near Lake Urumeya, and on the east of Assyria.

Since Sargon conquered Ullusunu king of Minni, there had been no direct war between the Mannians and Assyrians, and the only check they had received from Assyria was when Esarhaddon defeated the force they sent to the aid of the king of Azguza. Strengthened by the long peace, and finding the Assyrian army engaged elsewhere, the Mannians had engaged in a number of inroads into the Assyrian territory adjacent to them. The cities of Sar-igbi, Guzune, and others near Paddiri, which had formed part of the Assyrian empire, had been captured and colonized by them, and now formed part of the kingdom of Minni. It was necessary to put a stop to the Mannian incursions, and as soon as his army was at liberty, Assur-bani-pal ordered his troops to collect at Duran preparatory to marching against

Minni. From Duran the Assyrian army started for Minni, but meanwhile the king of Minni, Ahsera, had not been idle, he had assembled his army and gave directions to attack the Assyrian forces by night, in the hope of surprising and routing them. For this purpose he crossed the Assyrian frontier, expecting to find the Assyrian preparations incomplete, and by night he attacked the army of Assurbani-pal, but he met with a signal repulse, and his army was so utterly routed that it could not again take the field. For a space of twenty miles the battle-field was cumbered with the wrecks of the army of Ahsera, and the king fled to Izirtu the capital of Minni.

Assur-bani-pal now crossed the frontier in triumph, and commenced laying waste the Mannian territory. He captured in succession Aiusias, Halzia, Busutu, Sihua, and many other cities fell into the hands of the Assyrians, who destroyed them and carried off the people and goods. As Assur-bani-pal advanced towards the capital Izirtu, Ahsera abandoned the city and fled to a fortress, according to one document named Istatti, according to another Adrana. Assur-bani-pal now entered Izirtu, and captured all the cities round it, laying waste the country of Minni for fifteen days' journey. At this time the Assyrians retook the district of Paddiri, and the cities round it which had been conquered by the Mannians, and these districts were again annexed to Assyria. Assur-bani-pal conquered as far as the region of Arsiyanis in the highlands of Minni, and slew a Mannian general named Raidisadi. The Assyrians expelled the Mannians from the cities

near Assyria, and reoccupied them, then returned to
Assyria laden with booty.

The people of Minni were exasperated against
Ahsera their king for his ill success in the war, and
made a revolt against him, and surrounded the fortress
in which he had taken refuge. The attendants of the
king then murdered him, and threw his body outside
the city, where it was treated with great indignity.
The brothers and other relations of Ahsera shared the
same fate, but Valli one of his sons escaped, and
mounted his father's throne. Valli resolved to make
peace with Assyria, and sent his eldest son Erisinni at
the head of a deputation to Nineveh, to offer his
submission to Assur-bani-pal. The Assyrian monarch
demanded and received the daughter of Valli in
marriage, and appointed an additional annual tribute
of thirty horses.

Soon after Assur-bani-pal attacked the Medes, and
captured seventy-five of their towns, belonging to a
Median chief named Biriz-hadri, and to Sarati and
Paraza, sons of Gagi chief of the Saki.

An Assyrian general, the tartan or commander-
in-chief of the army, who ruled over a province
named Lubdi near the Babylonian frontier, named
Iludaria, about this time thought to make himself
independent, and attacked the district of Ubummi;
but while his forces lay encamped before the city of
Kullimir, the inhabitants sallied out in the night and
defeated them, killing Iludaria in the battle. The
inhabitants of Kullimir cut off the head of the rebel
general, and sent it to Nineveh to Assur-bani-pal.

The attention of Assur-bani-pal was now called to the

affairs of Elam. Ever since the reign of Sargon the Elamites had been the determined enemies of Assyria, they had encouraged and assisted every revolt against her, and their territory had been a refuge for every rebel.

In the earlier part of the reign of Esarhaddon, this policy had been reversed by Umman-aldas I, king of Elam, who refused to allow the son of Merodach-Baladan to take refuge there. Through his reign he adhered to the policy of peace with Assyria, and when his two brothers endeavoured to persuade him to invade Chaldea, he refused, and they being hostile to Assyria murdered him, and one of them named Urtaki took his throne. Urtaki, although he did not openly make war with Esarhaddon, allowed his brother Teumman to send his servant Zineni into Chaldea to try to persuade the people to revolt in favour of a man named Nabu-dimtir, probably a relative of Merodach-Baladan; but the Chaldean chiefs answered that Nahid-maruduk was their lord, and they were servants of the king of Assyria.

After this, early in the reign of Assur-bani-pal, there was a famine in Elam, and many of the Elamite tribes emigrated to Assyria to escape the drought. These fugitives Assur-bani-pal treated kindly, and allowed them to remain in Assyria until the rains recommenced in Elam, when they returned unmolested to their own country.

Forgetting this act, the king of Elam, Urtaki, meditated the invasion of Babylonia, and listening to the advice of his general Maruduk-zakir-ibni, he drew over to him Bel-basa the king of the Gambuli, and

Nabu-zakir-eres the governor of part of Chaldea, and joining his forces with theirs, broke into Babylonia.

Assur-bani-pal appears at first to have disbelieved this act of aggression, and he sent an officer to Babylonia to ascertain if it was true. His messenger returned and informed him that the Elamites were spread over the country like a flight of locusts, and that their camp was pitched against Babylon, from which place they were plundering in all directions. Roused by this intelligence, Assur-bani-pal at once assembled his army and marched into Babylonia against them. Urtaki on finding that Assur-bani-pal had advanced against him, collected his troops and retreated towards his own country, but he did not escape, for the Assyrian army came up with him near the frontier, and attacking his troops, drove them in confusion across the border.

Urtaki king of Elam was so mortified at this defeat that within a year he committed suicide, and the chiefs who had aided in the invasion, lived for some time in fear that Assur-bani-pal would take revenge for the attack on his dominions.

Assur-bani-pal appears to have been of an indolent disposition, and took no steps to avenge this invasion; and peace would most probably have continued if it had not been for a new provocation from Elam. On the death of Urtaki he was succeeded by his brother Teumman, who had always been the bitter enemy of Assyria, and the leader in every action against her interests.

The law of succession to the crown was the same in Elam as the old Turkish law, that is, on the death of a king, his brother succeeded in preference to his sons, and these latter had to wait until after the death of their uncles. Umman-aldas I had left sons, but they were passed over in favour of Urtaki, brother of Umman-aldas. Urtaki also left sons, but these were passed over in favour of Teumman. This law caused frequent changes among the rulers of Elam, and was a fruitful cause of strife. On the accession of Teumman, he was suspected of a design to change the law in favour of his own sons, and murder the sons of his two elder brothers, to clear the way for them. Fearing this, Umman-igas, Umman-appa, and Tammaritu, the three sons of Urtaki, Kudurru and Paru, sons of Umman-aldas, with sixty of the seed-royal and a large number of adherents, fled from Elam and came to Nineveh, where they became supplicants at the throne of Assur-bani-pal, and took service under him. Assur-bani-pal received the Elamite princes with royal favours, promised them protection and assistance, and they attended him on state occasions.

Teumman, who was of a restless but determined character, and bent on war, could not brook to see his nephews received with honour by the Assyrian monarch, and determined to attempt to obtain possession of them. He appears to have despised the personal prowess of Assur-bani-pal, most of whose victories had been gained by his generals, while he spent his time in luxury at Nineveh.

Teumman sent two of his officers, Umbadara and Nabudamiq, with a message to Assur-bani-pal at Nineveh, demanding that the king of Assyria should surrender to him the fugitives. Assur-bani-pal refused this, and both parties felt they were on the eve of a serious crisis. The Elamites were the most powerful and warlike enemies of Assyria, and they owed their past defeats in great measure to the unwarlike character of the sovereigns who had led them, but now they were ruled by a man whose bravery and ferocity were known, and who was determined to embrace the first opportunity of measuring his strength with Assyria. Assur-bani-pal himself attached the greatest importance to the events of the coming struggle, for no one of his other wars is so often repeated on the sculptures, or mentioned so frequently in the inscriptions. In the month Tammuz, while every one expected the outbreak of hostilities, there was a darkness in the morning which obscured the rising sun, and which some suppose to have been an eclipse. This event was eagerly seized upon by the Assyrian astrologers, and declared to be an omen that the king of Elam should be killed and his country destroyed. In the nexth month the Elamite sovereign gathered his army, while Assur-bani-pal, who was very superstitious, was engaged in celebrating splendid rites to the Lady of Arbela, the goddess of war and battle. As the Assyrian monarch was in the midst of these ceremonies, word was brought to him that Teumman had vowed that he would not rest until he had fought with Assur-bani-pal. On receiving this message Assur-bani-pal went into the sanctuary of Ishtar, and his conduct forms a striking parallel with that of Hezekiah, when he received the message of Sennacherib. The Assyrian monarch approached the goddess, he wept before her, he reminded her of his good deeds in

restoring the temples, professed that he loved her
courts, and went to worship her; he contrasted the
conduct of Teumman the violent man, hater of the
gods; he related all her titles and glories, told how
Teumman gathered his army against him, and wound
up by imploring her to hurl him down like a stone in
the day of battle, and sweep him away like a storm and
evil wind. Assur-bani-pal relates that the goddess
heard his prayer, and told him not to fear, and in the
same night, while a seer slept he had a vision, and the
goddess appeared to him, surrounded with glory,
holding a bow in her hand, and equipped ready for
war. She sent Assur-bani-pal an encouraging message,
and told him to eat food, drink wine, and engage in
festivities, for she would give him the victory.

Trusting to the message of Ishtar, in the following
month Elul, Assur-bani-pal collected his troops, and
went to the city of Duran to start the expedition.

Teumman king of Elam had been earlier in collecting his troops, which he took to Bit-imbi, on the
border of Elam; but here occurred a fatal delay; instead of advancing into Assyria, he lay at Bit-imbi
until the Assyrian army arrived opposite him at
Duran.

Teumman, when he saw the strength of the Assyrian
forces which were encamped at Duran, feared to risk
a battle with them there, and retired to the neighbourhood of Shushan his capital, where he fixed on a
strong position, with his front protected by the river
Ulai. The army of Assur-bani-pal followed the re-
treating Elamites, and the retrograde movement of
Teumman began to have a bad effect on his followers,

his life is said to have been in danger, and he made a
promise of gold to the soldiers to pacify them.

Assur-bani-pal had fixed on Umman-igas, son of
the late king Urtaki, as his candidate for the throne of
Elam, and the young prince accompanied the army
into Elam, helping to draw over some of the Elamites
to the Assyrian side.

Simburu an Elamite chief, seeing the fortune of war
was likely to be favourable to Assyria, now abandoned
Teumman, and came into the Assyrian camp. Umba-
kidinna and Zineni, two other chiefs, also left the
Elamite camp, and to make their presence more
acceptable to Assur-bani-pal, they murdered some of
the Elamite princes, and brought their heads to the
Assyrians. These defections weakened the force of
Teumman, and he now became anxious to treat with
Assur-bani-pal, and for this purpose he sent out to the
Assyrian monarch one of his generals named Ituni.
Assur-bani-pal refused to listen to any terms, and at
once ordered his troops to attack. The Assyrians
crossed the Ulai, and attacked the camp of the
Elamites on the first day of the month Tisri. The
superiority of their archers soon became apparent,
although the bow was the national weapon of the
Elamites. The Elamite army began to give way, and
the battle ended in their total rout. Ituni the
messenger of Teumman was in the camp of the
Assyrians, and seeing the rout of the Elamites, drew
his sword and cut in two his own bow in token of
his despair.

Urtaki, a relative of Teumman, and one of his
generals being badly wounded in the battle, called to

one of the Assyrians and asked him to despatch him, and take his head to Assur-bani-pal.

Teumman, who was in the thickest of the battle, was accompanied by his eldest son; when he saw the overthrow of his hopes and rout of his army, he tore his beard in his grief, and fled from the scene. At this moment he was struck by an Assyrian arrow, and supported by his son, he rode in his chariot to reach some woods near the Elamite position, which would be a shelter against the Assyrians. The chariot of the king was overturned in the confusion, and Teumman and his son thrown to the ground. Tamritu the son of Teumman now dragged his wounded father out of the melée, and when the Assyrians came up he stood over him to protect him, but his efforts were unavailing, and they were both captured and their heads cut off.

Assur-bani-pal now sent a general into the town of Shushan, near which the battle was fought, and with him Umman-igas the Elamite prince. The Assyrian general proclaimed Umman-igas king of Elam, and with the wrecks of their army scattered over the plain, and the river Ulai choked with the corpses of their soldiers, the people had to come out and do homage to the new ruler forced upon them by the Assyrian monarch. Tammaritu, the youngest brother of Umman-igas, a man of artful address, had gained very much on the opinion of Assur-bani-pal, and he was at the same time made sub-king of the district of Hidalu, a mountainous part in the east of Elam.

The next work of the Assyrian army was to punish the people of Gambuli, who dwelt in the marshes near the mouth of the Tigris. The Gambuli had for some

years been close allies of the Elamites, and had aided
them in their attacks against Assur-bani-pal, both in the
days of Urtaki and in the war with Teumman. The
capital of Gambuli was a city named Sapi-bel, a place
which had been fortified by Esarhaddon, and lay in
the midst of difficult marshes. The Assyrians came
down on Gambuli like a storm, captured Sapi-bel, and
destroyed it, overthrowing the fortifications and sinking
them into the marsh. Vast numbers of prisoners and
spoil in abundance were carried off. Dunanu the king
of Gambuli, and Samgunu his brother, Mannukiahi
and Nabuuzilli, two of their officers, and Paliya son of
Nabu-sapau and grandson of Merodach-Baladan, were
among the prisoners.

The Assyrian army now commenced its journey
home, with its prisoners, its ghastly trophies, and its
spoil. The royal procession moved into Nineveh by
the grand gate of the city, which was on the Baghdad
road. Assur-bani-pal in his triumphal chariot led his
warriors, attended by musicians playing on their instruments, followed by the unfortunate prisoners; first
came Dunanu the captured king of Gambuli; round his
neck was a cord, and attached to it hung in front of
his breast, the severed head of Teumman king of
Elam; after Dunanu came his brother Samgunu, and
hung round his neck in a similar manner was the head
of Tamritu, the son of the Elamite monarch.

In the hour of his triumph an embassy entered
Arbela from Armenia. Rusa king of Armenia, a
country traditionally hostile to Assyria, had heard of
the triumph of Assur-bani-pal, and how he had crushed
the power of Elam; he thought it advisable to make
peace with him, and sent two of his officers to Assyria.

to congratulate Assur-bani-pal on his victories. The Assyrian monarch, desirous of showing his power to the Armenian envoys, caused the Elamite envoys, Umbadara and Nabudamiq, to be brought out chained, and tortured in their presence. Umbadara and Nabudamiq had been sent by Teumman to Nineveh on a mission before the war, and Assur-bani-pal had put them in prison, and kept them there ever since. These two envoys, seeing the triumphal procession enter the city and the decapitated head of their monarch among the trophies, were transported with grief. Umbadara tore his beard, and Nabudamiq drawing his sword, ran himself through the body and expired.

The work of torturing the prisoners now commenced. Dunanu and some of the principal prisoners were pinned to the ground by four stakes, their tongues pulled out, and then their skins flayed off. Paliya and some others had their limbs cut off: all were put to death with great cruelty, and at the close of the work the head of Teumman was raised to the top of the great gate of Nineveh, that all the people might see it: such was Nineveh, which the prophet Nahum truly calls a bloody city.

For a little time there was peace in the Assyrian empire, and Assur-bani-pal again pursued his round of pleasures at Nineveh, but soon troubles began to appear in Babylonia.

Assur-bani-pal had been made king of Assyria during the life of his father, and Saulmugina, another son of Esarhaddon, was on the death of that monarch in B.C. 668, made king at Babylon, in subordination to his brother Assur-bani-pal. The Assyrian monarch, although he had given Babylon to his brother, kept a tight

hold on the country.   He placed garrisons in the principal fortresses, and appointed the provincial governors.
Thus Saulmugina had little but the name of sovereign,
and had to address his brother as "the king my lord."
Neither Saulmugina nor his subjects were satisfied with
this position, and it became evident that a revolt was
imminent.   Assur-bani-pal was kept well informed of the

Torture of Captives.

state of affairs by the constant reports of his officers,
and particularly by the letters sent from Kudur,
governor of Uruk or Erech (modern Warka), who was
one of the most active and intelligent of these commanders.

Assur-bani-pal foreseeing the coming storm, issued a
proclamation to the Babylonians, reminding them of

the ancient friendship between Assyria and their country, and exhorting them to be faithful ;—but in the same year the revolt broke out.

Saulmugina determined to make himself independent, and sent messengers to the Chaldeans, the Elamites, Arabians, and others, pressing them to join in the revolt; at the same time he sent a deputation to Assur-bani-pal to assure him of his continued devotion, and thus throw dust in his eyes while the preparations for revolt were completing. Assur-bani-pal received the embassy of his brother with many marks of favour, and did not betray any suspicion of his object.

Meanwhile Saulmugina sent ambassadors to the Chaldeans in the south of Babylonia, and tried to induce them to revolt; these messengers arrived at the town of Ur, and some of the people revolted. At first Sintabniuzur, governor of Ur, was faithful, but afterwards he himself joined the movement. Kudur, governor of Erech, then procured a reinforcement from Paliya governor of Arapha, and went down to Ur to stop the revolt, but he was not strong enough to effect anything. The greatest ally Saulmugina gained in this direction was Nabu-bel-zikri, the grandson of Merodach-Baladan, a chief who inherited the hatred of his grandfather for the Assyrians. Nabu-bel-zikri seized the Assyrians in his region near the sea coast, and put them in bonds.

Saulmugina sent messengers to Umman-igas king of Elam, who owed his kingdom to Assur-bani-pal, and pressed him to revolt, tempting him by a present of gold and silver, taken from the principal Babylonian temples. Umman-igas, forgetting all the benefits he had received from Assur-bani-pal, joined in the scheme

of Saulmugina, and revolting against Assyria, gathered
an army to send into Babylonia to the aid of the
brother of Assur-bani-pal. The Elamite army was committed to the care of Undasi, son of the late king
Teumman, Zazaz governor of Billate, Paru lord of
Hilmu, Attamitu commander of the archers, and Nesu
general of the foot soldiers; and Umman-igas endeavoured to stimulate Undasi, by calling on him to
avenge the death of his father against Assyria. The
Elamite generals started with the messengers of Saulmugina for Babylonia, and when they arrived in that
country attacked the forces of Assur-bani-pal in Chaldea.
The Assyrian generals defeated the Elamites, killed Attamitu and sent his head to Assur-bani-pal; but their
forces were not strong enough to subdue the revolt
which had spread over the whole south of the empire.

Retribution was soon to follow Umman-igas. After
the defeat of his forces in Chaldea, his nephew, named
Tammaritu, raised a rebellion against him, and defeated
him in a pitched battle, he then cut off the head of
Umman-igas and took his crown.

Saulmugina, still anxious for the support of the
Elamites, sent an embassy with fresh presents to
Tammaritu, and the new king of Elam listened to
his appeal and marched at the head of his troops into
Babylonia. While Tammaritu was in Babylonia a
conspiracy was preparing against him; Indabigas one
of his servants set himself up as king at Shushan, and
defeating the followers of Tammaritu who were left in
the country, marched against Tammaritu himself.
Tammaritu was also in his turn defeated, and fled to
the sea coast with the remnant of the royal family of
Elam. These civil wars were ruining the cause of

the insurrection and reducing Babylonia and Elam to
a state of anarchy, added to which a famine took place
and increased the miseries of the people.

Just at this time Assur-bani-pal moved fresh reinforce-
ments into Babylonia, and commenced a vigorous
campaign against the rebels.   The Assyrians defeated
the combined forces of the Babylonians, Elamites,
Chaldeans, Arabians and others, and shut them up in
the four cities, Babylon, Sippara, Borsippa and Cutha.
The siege of these places was prosecuted with vigour,
and the people were reduced to such straits that they
eat their children from famine.   The great Babylonian
cities fell, and Saulmugina, seeing that Babylon was
taken, burnt himself in his palace to avoid falling into
the hands of his brother.

The officers of the king of Assyria had now no
difficulty in trampling out the remains of the rebellion,
after which Assur-bani-pal reconstituted the government
and restored as much as possible the institutions which
were in force before the revolt, only taking care to
bind Babylonia more firmly to Assyria.

While the events were going on, Tammaritu, who
fled before Indabigas and took ship on the Persian
Gulf, met with heavy weather and was wrecked; he
then gave himself up to Maruduk-sar-uzur an Assyrian
officer, having received promise of protection from
Assur-bani-pal.   Maruduk-sar-uzur passed him on to
Bel-ibni, who sent him to Assyria.

Mannu-ki-babil of Dakkuri, Hea-mubasa of Amukkan, Nadan of Pekod and various other smaller governors were punished for complicity in the revolt, but
Nabu-bel-zikri fled from Chaldea and found refuge at
the court of Indabigas king of Elam.

CHAPTER XIV.

REIGN OF ASSUR-BANI-PAL FROM THE CONQUEST OF

BABYLON UNTIL HIS DEATH, B. C. 648–626.

PEACE was now again restored, but the frontiers of the empire were much reduced; Elam was independent on the east, Arabia on the south, and Egypt on the west. Indabigas king of Elam, seeing the failure of the Babylonian revolt, was anxious to make his peace with Assur-bani-pal, and for this purpose sent an embassy to Nineveh; but the Assyrian monarch at once demanded the surrender of Nabu-bel-zikri and the Assyrians whom he had taken with him, and threatened if they were not given up, to invade Elam, destroy the principal towns, carry off the people, depose Indabigas, and set up in his place another monarch. As this threat was couched in violent language, the Elamite envoy feared to deliver it to his master, and Assur-bani-pal sent a messenger of his own to Indabigas. The Assyrian envoy arrived at Deri or Duran, when he heard that a revolution had taken place in Elam. Umman-aldas son of the general Attamitu, who had been killed in battle with the Assyrians, revolted against Indabigas and defeated him in battle. Indabigas and his family were killed, and Umman-aldas seated himself on his throne. Elam now became the theatre of civil war, for considerable parts of the country refused to submit to Umman-aldas, and the standard of revolt was raised by Umman-igas, whose father Umbadara had been a prisoner at Nineveh. The forces of Umman-aldas II and Umman-igas joined battle by the banks of the river Huthut, and Umman-aldas gained the victory ; two other claimants for the crown now started up, Umbagua and Pahe, these held out in the interior of the country until the reconquest of Elam by the Assyrians.

As soon as Umman-aldas was seated on the throne a messenger arrived demanding the surrender of Nabu-bel-zikri, and the Chaldean prince fearing he should be delivered up to the king of Assyria, and tired of his life of danger and exile, called on his armour-bearer to despatch him, and they together ran themselves through with their swords. Nabu-bil-zikri was the last of the family of Merodach-Baladan, a family which had played an important part in Babylonia for the last 100 years.

Umman-aldas now gave the corpse of the Babylonian prince, the head of his armour-bearer, and some of the other fugitives alive, to the messenger of Assur-bani-pal, and they were presented before the king at Nineveh.

Soon after this Assur-bani-pal determined on a new expedition against Elam to dethrone Umman-aldas, and set up Tammaritu the former monarch in his place.

Umman-aldas had expected the invasion, and to be prepared for it he had strengthened Bit-imbi a fortress on the frontier between Assyria and Elam. Bit-imbi had been captured and destroyed by Sennacherib, but Umman-aldas had restored the town, and built new and stronger walls, garrisoned it with troops, and placed it under the command of a relative of his own, Imbaappi. On the starting of the Assyrian expedition a number of Elamite tribes from places near Assyria, went over to Assur-bani-pal and voluntarily took the service of Assyria, by which means they protected themselves and their property, as laying near the border, they were exposed to great danger in every invasion.

Crossing the frontier of Elam Assur-bani-pal attacked and captured Bit-imbi, and he put the garrison to the sword, because of the resistance he met with; Imba-appi the commander was captured, and sent in chains to Nineveh, and in the fort the Assyrians found the queen of the late Elamite king Teumman and some of his children, who were sent prisoners to Assyria.

Umman-aldas king of Elam was in his capital Madaktu when he heard of the capture of Bit-imbi, and he at once fled to the mountains, abandoning the city to the Assyrians. Umbagua, the opponent of Umman-aldas, who ruled in the city of Bubilu, also fled on the approach of the Assyrians, and crossing the sea abandoned the country. The Assyrian army then advanced to Shushan and there they proclaimed Tammaritu once more as king of Elam ; he agreeing to acknowledge Assur-bani-pal as his lord, and to pay tribute to Assyria.

Scarcely was Tammaritu seated on the throne, when he began to plot the destruction of the Assyrian army which had placed him there and now garrisoned his city. In this design he was foiled, and Assur-bani-pal deposed him and imprisoned him. The Assyrian army now passed through the country carrying fire and sword wherever they went, and plundering the people, but no settled government was set up, and no permanent conquest effected until after the Assyrian army had retired, when Umman-aldas returned from the mountains and resumed the government of the country.

Assur-bani-pal after this set out once more to attack the Elamites, determining this time to subjugate the country entirely, and incorporate it with Assyria. The pretext for this, the third invasion of the country, was, that the Elamites refused to deliver up an image of the goddess Nana, which a former Elamite king had carried away from Babylonia.

Starting from Assyria Assur-bani-pal once more captured Bit-imbi, and then overran the districts of Rasi and Hamanu. Umman-aldas, hearing of the invasion, once more left his capital Madaktu, and retired to the city of Dur-undasi. Near here there was a stream called the Itite suitable for defence, and here Umman-aldas resolved to make a stand. The Assyrian army pressed on after him, and took in succession Madaktu, Haltemas, Shushan, Bubilu and various other towns, ending with the capture of Dur-undasi.

The Assyrians now saw before them the river Itite in full flood, and the other bank of the stream lined by the warriors of Umman-aldas, waiting to make a last desperate stand for independence. The Assyrian soldiers wavered and feared to cross the stream, but it

was said that the goddess Ishtar had appeared in the
night, and promised to march in front of them and
assure them the victory. This relation inspired the
troops, and they crossed the river in face of the
Elamites, storming their camp and gaining a complete
victory. Numbers of the Elamites fell, and Umman-
aldas fled once more to the mountains. After this
there was no open resistance, and the Assyrian soldiers
carried destruction everywhere. The annals now record city after city captured and destroyed, and whole
districts reduced to the condition of a desert.

   The city of Shushan, the ancient capital of the
country and the high place of the Elamite worship,
was plundered and destroyed.   Assur-bani-pal entered
into its palace in triumph, and broke open the treasure
house;   here was a store of gold, silver, precious
stones, furniture and other things, partly the spoil of
various conquests of the Elamite kings, and partly
gifts from surrounding nations, for the assistance of
the Elamites.   All these things were brought out and
carried off, arms, horses, chariots and trappings of war
were removed, the great tower of Shushan was broken
down, and the Assyrian monarch penetrated into the
holy of holies of the Susians, where was the image
of their great national god, whom no man was supposed to look upon.   This image and those of various
other gods and kings, were carried away to Assyria.
The whole city was committed to the flames, and
nothing left worth removing.   Assur-bani-pal brought
out in triumph the image of Nana goddess of Erech,
which Kudur-nanhundi, a former Elamite king, had
carried to Shushan, and which was said to have been

worshipped for 1635 years. On the first day of the month Kislev the image was restored to its temple in Erech with great rejoicing.

Pahe, an Elamite who had claimed the crown against Umman-aldas, now submitted to Assur-bani-pal and was carried to Nineveh by the Assyrians, who returned to their country after making Elam a desert.

The records of Assur-bani-pal now travel back several years, to take up the history of Arabia. Vaiteh king of Arabia had succeeded to the throne during the reign of Esarhaddon, and was on the throne at the time of the accession of Assur-bani-pal. In regard to him one of Assur-bani-pal's records shows a curious disregard of history, boldly transferring the incident of the embassy to pray for the Arabian gods from his father's reign to his own (see p. 132). Assur-bani-pal professes to have been very friendly to the king of Arabia, and to have conferred numerous benefits upon him, but Vaiteh was guilty of ingratitude, and when Saulmugina revolted against his brother, the Arabian monarch received his envoys and joined the rebels.

It appears to have been the purpose of Vaiteh to carve himself out an empire during the struggle between Assyria and her dependencies, and for this purpose he divided his army into two portions ; one of these he placed under the command of Abiyateh and Aimu, two brothers, the sons of Tehar, and sent them to assist Saulmugina at Babylon, while the other and main portion of his army he took charge of himself, and with it invaded Palestine. Adiya a warlike woman, the wife of Vaiteh and queen of Arabia, went with this force, and Ammuladi king of Kedar was another prince who joined, probably being a tributary of Vaiteh.

Vaiteh at first seemed to carry all before him; he invaded Hezron, Hirataqaza, Edom, Yabrud, Beth-ammon, Hauran, Moab, Saharri, Harge and Zobah. The enumeration of the places attacked shows that his army passed up through Edom, then Moab and Ammon, then to Hauran or Bashan, reaching Zobah. Here however he was checked; the Assyrian generals in Syria met his forces and defeated them, and drove his troops in succession out of all these places. The Arabs were slaughtered in considerable numbers, and Vaiteh fled away to the land of Nabatea.

Nathan king of Nabatea looked with disfavour upon the fugitive, and reminded him that he could not protect him against Assyria, and soon afterwards we find him a prisoner in the hands of Assur-bani-pal, but we do not know in what way he was taken. On being brought to Nineveh, Vaiteh was kept by Assur-bani-pal a prisoner among his hounds, in the park on the east of Nineveh.

Ammuladi king of Kedar had joined Vaiteh in the invasion of Palestine, and shared at first in the spoil of the conquests, but his career was stopped by Kamas-halta king of Moab, who was faithful to Assur-bani-pal. The Moabite monarch defeated Ammuladi in battle, and capturing him, sent him in chains to Nineveh. Ammuladi was treated by Assur-bani-pal in the same manner as Vaiteh, being placed prisoner with the hounds in the royal park.

Adiya queen of Arabia shared a similar fate; she was defeated with a detachment of Arabs by a general of Assur-bani-pal, and fell into the hands of the Assyrians, who sent her also a prisoner to Nineveh. Thus the expedition to Syria entirely collapsed after overrunning so much of the country; and the king of the Nabateans seeing the triumph of Assur-bani-pal, sent a messenger to Nineveh, and made submission to the Assyrian monarch.

The other wing of the Arabian army, under the leadership of Abiyateh and Aimu, marched to Babylon and joined the forces of Saulmugina. The allied army was met and defeated by the Assyrians, and they were driven into the city of Babylon, where they were besieged by the Assyrian forces. After a time the famine in the city became so severe that the defenders of the place eat human flesh to satisfy their hunger, and the Arabians resolved to attempt to cut their way out of the blockade and escape. For this purpose they sallied out, and threw themselves upon the Assyrians; but their attempt was repulsed, and they were driven back into the city. Now Abiyateh came out and surrendered to the Assyrian commander, and offered to take service under Assur-bani-pal. The Assyrian general sent him to Assur-bani-pal at Nineveh, and there he swore by the great gods to be faithful to Assyria. At this time Vaiteh king of Arabia was a prisoner at Nineveh, and Assur-bani-pal accepting the submission of Abiyateh, proclaimed him king of Arabia instead of Vaiteh, and sent him to take possession of the country. Meanwhile the people of Arabia seeing their king was a prisoner at Nineveh, proceeded to elect another monarch to fill his throne, and their choice fell upon another prince named Vaiteh, who was son of Bir-dada and nephew of the last monarch. Abiyateh on his return from Nineveh agreed to share the government with Vaiteh II, and they then sent an embassy to Nathan king of Nabatea, asking him to join them against Assyria. In spite of his recent submission to Assyria, Nathan readily joined them, and the three princes then attacked the Assyrian provinces in their vicinity. Bands of Arab plunderers spread themselves along the edges of the desert, and laid waste all the Assyrian borders. These parties were difficult to follow, and their incursions were only checked in one place, to break out in another.

Under these circumstances Assur-bani-pal prepared a great expedition to penetrate into Arabia, and punish the kings in their own territories. The expedition of Assur-bani-pal crossed the Tigris from Nineveh, and marched to the Euphrates, then passing this river at the time of the spring flood, they crossed a region of extensive forests, and came to the desert of Vas, the first region of the enemy; this was an arid, desolate plain, where no bird had made its nest, and even the wild ass of the desert was not found.

The forces of Vaiteh II, Abiyateh, and Nathan the Nabatean, at home here, retired before the Assyrians, who marched a distance from Nineveh of 100 kaspu, or from 600 to 700 miles.

The army of Assur-bani-pal weary with thirst, arrived at a city named Hadatta, and on the twenty-fifth day of Sivan departed from Hadatta and marched to a city called Laribda, a place with a stone tower, and what was of more consequence to the troops, a good spring of water. After a rest here the Assyrian commanders

struck again into the desert, which was as arid and
desolate as the former portion; neither bird nor beast
was seen. At length the troops came to a small
collection of towns, Hurarina, Yarki, and Aialla.
Here the Arabians resolved to make a stand, and the
Assyrians found the forces of the Isammih, the wor-
shippers of Adarsamain, the national deity of the
Arabians, and the Nabateans; these they defeated
and captured numbers of prisoners, besides asses,
camels and sheep. The scene of the battle was about
fifty miles from Aialla, and the Assyrian army had to
return to that city to procure water. Starting again
from Aialla, the Assyrians marched about forty miles
to a place called Qurazitu, where they fell in with the
forces of Vaiteh son of Bir-dadda. The king himself
escaped, but his sisters, his wife and family, with
numbers of prisoners and cattle, camels, asses, and
sheep, fell into their hands. The Assyrians now laden
with spoil, turned back and took the road to Damascus
where they deposited their booty, and again started
out against the Arabs. From Damascus they at once
struck into the desert on the third day of Ab, and
after a march of forty miles came to Hulhuliti, from
there they went to Hukkurana where another battle
took place, and Abiyateh was captured alive, and sent
bound hand and foot to Assyria, The fugitives from
this battle took refuge in the city of Lanhabbi, where
they were followed by the Assyrians, and in a subsequent
engagement Aimu, brother of Abiyateh, was captured.
He was sent to Nineveh where he was flayed alive.

The army of Assur-bani-pal returning from the
Arabian war, passed through Palestine and punished

some of the cities which had revolted during these
troubles. Usu or Hosah near Tyre had refused its
tribute; severe punishment was inflicted on it, and the
deities and people of the place carried captive; Accho
which had revolted received similar treatment, the
rebels being sent to Assyria. Immense numbers of
captives and cattle, the spoils of Arabia were carried
to Assyria after the war, and camels were so plentiful
that they were sold for half a shekel of silver in the
gate of Nineveh.

The Assyrian invasion of Arabia, and the driving
away of the flocks and herds of the people, produced
a severe famine, and the Assyrian annals represent the
Arabians as saying one to another, that all these
troubles had fallen upon them, because they had rebelled against the empire of Assur-bani-pal.

Some time later than this a general of Assur-bani-pal
forwarded the news to the king of Assyria at Nineveh,
that a chief named Aikamaru, son of Ammihitah of
Vas, had gone down and attacked the Nabateans and
destroyed them. Only one man escaped, and him he
sent on to Nineveh that the king of Assyria might
learn from his lips of the matter.

After the successful close of the Arabian campaign,
another triumph was in store for the Assyrian monarch.
When the Assyrian army retired after the third campaign against Elam, Umman-aldas resumed his throne,
but the people of the country rose against him, and
compelled him once more to fly to the mountains,
where he was captured by the agents of Assur-bani-pal
and brought to Nineveh.

Assur-bani-pal had now regained most of his

dominions, and resolved on celebrating a great triumph at Nineveh. He ordered splendid sacrifices to be offered to the gods in the various temples, and then had his state chariot brought out, and Tammaritu, Pahe, and Umman-aldas, the three captive Elamite kings, and Vaiteh king of Arabia, fastened to the yoke. The king of Assyria then mounted his chariot, and the four captive monarchs were compelled to drag the carriage to the gate of the great temple of Ishtar. Here Assur-bani-pal alighted, and bowing his face to the ground, adored his divinities, and ascribed to Assur and Ishtar, and the whole train of his idols, his victories over his enemies.

Here the annals of this great monarch terminate, but he continued to reign for some years after the date of his last recorded campaigns, and died most probably about B.C. 626.

In the last and unknown portion of his reign at least one campaign took place; he went up again against the city of Tyre, deposed the king, and appointed an Assyrian governor in his place.

During the latter part of his reign there was constant war with the Egyptians, now reviving under the government of Psammitichus, and in the east the great Median power was growing, which was destined one day to overthrow Assyria itself.

CHAPTER XV.

THE public works of Assur-bani-pal were, as might be expected from the importance of his reign, grand. The principal of these was a noble palace on the platform of Koyunjik at Nineveh, now called the North Palace. There were no great bulls at the doorways, or gigantic winged figures, and the size of the sculpture in general was smaller than the sculpture of the other palaces; but there is a degree of beauty and spirit about the figures which more than compensates for this, and makes it the finest building raised by the Assyrians.

The principal scenes represented were hunting and banqueting parties, processions, and shows; few political events are celebrated on its walls, and the palace itself was rather a private building of the king, intended for his pleasure and his harem.

Assur-bani-pal also made some repairs to the palace of Sennacherib at Koyunjik, but here he was guilty of clearing the sculpture from the walls of the chambers and substituting his own.

He also restored the ramparts and walls of Nineveh, which had decayed since the time of Sennacherib.

At the city of Assur, the old capital of the country, he restored with great splendour the national temple called Sadi-matuti.

At Babylon he restored the temple of Bel and presented a splendid chariot and couch to the deity; various temples at Babylon, Nineveh, Harran, and other cities, he restored and beautified. Assur-bani-pal was devoted to the worship of the two Ishtars, and restored the temple of Ishtar at Nineveh, and with greater splendour the temple of Ishtar at Arbela. He also rebuilt the temple of Nergal at Tarbezi.

The grandest work of Assur-bani-pal was, however, not the building of palaces or temples, but the institu-

Inscribed Clay Tablet.

tion of the great library at Koyunjik. Collections of inscribed tablets had been made by Tiglath-Pileser II, king of Assyria B.C. 745, who had copied some historical inscriptions of his predecessors. Sargon, the founder of the dynasty to which Assur-bani-pal belonged, B.C. 722, had increased this library by adding a collection of astrological and similar texts, and Sennacherib, B.C. 705, had composed copies of the Assyrian canon, short histories, and miscellaneous inscriptions, to add to the collection. Sennacherib also moved the library from Calah, its original seat,

to Nineveh the capital.   Esarhaddon, b.c. 681, added
numerous historical and mythological texts.

All the inscriptions of the former kings were, however, nothing compared to those written during the reign
of Assur-bani-pal. Thousands of inscribed tablets from
all places, and on every variety of subject, were collected, and copied, and stored in the library of the
palace at Nineveh during his reign ; and by his state-

Scribes Writing.

ments they appear to have been intended for the in-
spection of the people, and to spread learning among
the Assyrians.   Among these tablets one class consisted of historical texts, some the histories of the
former kings of Assyria, and others copies of royal
inscriptions from various other places.

Similar to these were the copies of treaties, despatches, and orders from the king to his generals and

ministers, a large number of which formed part of the library.

There was a large collection of letters of all sorts, from despatches to the king on the one hand, down to private notes on the other.

Geography found a place among the sciences, and was represented by lists of countries, towns, rivers, and mountains, notices of the position, products, and character of districts, &c. &c.

There were tables giving accounts of the law and legal decisions, and tablets with contracts, loans, deeds of sale and barter, &c.

There were lists of tribute and taxes, accounts of property in the various cities, forming some approach to a census and general account of the empire.

One large and important section of the library was devoted to legends of various sorts, many of which were borrowed from other countries. Among these were the legends of the hero Izdubar, perhaps the Nimrod of the Bible. One of these legends gives the Chaldean account of the flood, others of this description give various fables and stories of evil spirits.

The mythological part of the library embraced lists of the gods, their titles, attributes, temples &c., hymns in praise of various deities, prayers to be used by different classes of men to different gods, and under various circumstances, as during eclipses or calamities, on setting out for a campaign, &c. &c.

Astronomy was represented by various tablets and works on the appearance and motions of the heavens, and the various celestial phenomena. Astrology was closely connected with astronomy, and formed a numerous class of subjects and inscriptions.

An interesting division was formed by the works on natural history; these consisted of lists of animals, birds, reptiles, trees, grasses, stones, &c. &c., arranged in classes, according to their character and affinities as then understood, lists of minerals and their uses, lists of foods, &c. &c.

Mathematics and arithmetic were found, including square and cube root, the working out of problems, &c. &c.

Much of the learning on these tablets was borrowed from the Chaldeans and people of Babylon, and had originally been written in a different language and style of writing, hence it was necessary to have translations and explanations of many of these; and in order to make their meaning clear, grammars, dictionaries, and lexicons were prepared, embracing the principal features of the two languages involved, and enabling the Assyrians to study the older inscriptions.

Such are some of the principal features of the grand Assyrian library, which Assur-bani-pal established at Nineveh, and which probably numbered over 10,000 clay documents.

Assur-bani-pal was known to the Greeks under the name of Sardanapalus, and they have represented him as soft and effeminate, living surrounded by women and eunuchs, adopting extravagant dress, and indulging in sensual pleasure and the enjoyment of the luxuries of the table. The picture drawn by the Greek writers is only partially true; certainly Assur-bani-pal increased the royal harem, and gave great splendour to the building in which his wives resided; the king is also represented in his own sculpture reclining on a couch beside his queen, drinking wine and partaking of a banquet spread before him in the royal gardens, under the shadow of beautiful trees; while the royal musicians are standing round playing on their instruments, and fan-bearers make cool breezes round his couch; but this is only part of his character. Assur-bani-pal was passionately fond of the chase, and had a royal park on the eastern side of Nineveh, where various wild animals were kept enclosed that the king might have the opportunity of hunting them; lions, wild asses, gazelles and birds, were the principal objects of his sport, and for carrying it on he kept a noble breed of hounds, to which particular attention was paid.

In common with all his people, Assur-bani-pal was steeped in cruelty and superstition; his devotion to his gods was slavish, and his gifts to their temples rich.

As a soldier Assur-bani-pal did little to distinguish himself, if he ever accompanied his army it was rather as a spectator than a commander, the administration of military affairs being in the hands of skilful and competent generals. The king, however, took the glory of every triumph to his arms, and pleased his people with shows and pageants, of which he was very fond. Although he was inferior to his father in the genius that builds up an empire, he kept together all his father's possessions except Egypt, and added to them the conquest of Elam; and he ruled the empire with a gorgeous pomp, which was gratifying to the pride of his subjects.

In spite of the flourishing state of art and learning, and the show of strength made during the reign of Assur-bani-pal, decay had set in at the heart of the empire, and it was hastening to a rapid and signal fall.

CHAPTER XVI.

AFTER the death of Assur-bani-pal Assyrian history is involved in some obscurity, and the succession of the kings is uncertain. At this time several of the surrounding nations were rising into importance, while Assyria experienced a serious decline.

Psammitichus, king of Egypt, who had established himself during the reign of Assur-bani-pal, had ever since been a determined enemy of Assyria. After the retreat of the army of Assur-bani-pal Psammitichus commenced to attack the Philistine cities; he stormed Gaza and laid siege to Ashdod, which siege lasted for twenty-nine years. On the death of Psammitichus, B.C. 612, his son, Necho II, inherited his crown, and continued the war with Assyria.

On the east of Assyria remarkable changes were taking place. The tribes of the Medes, occupying a wild and sterile country, were organising themselves into a great power. For two hundred years the Medes had been partially under Assyrian dominion, Shalmaneser II, Vul-nirari III, Tiglath Pileser II, Sargon, Esarhaddon, and other Assyrian monarchs had successively invaded their territory, and taken tribute from them, and although their population was

numerous and warlike, the state of division in which
they were always found, rendered them powerless to
resist these attacks. The principal tribes of the Medes
beginning to realise this fact, and endeavouring to
escape from the state of lawlessness in which they
lived, submitted to the power of a man named Diakku
or Dejoices, son of Phraortes, who was probably
hereditary chief of one of the tribes. The great wars
undertaken by Assur-bani-pal against Egypt, Babylonia,
and Elam, caused the growth of the new power to
be neglected, and the conquest and crushing of the
Elamite power on the south of Media opened a way
for the spread of the kingdom of Dejoices. Dejoices
firmly established his power, and left his dominions
to his son Phraortes about B.C. 650. Phraortes added
to the dominions of his father, and conquered the
country of the Persians, a kindred race living south
of the Medes.

The death of Assur-bani-pal. B.C. 626, gave the opportunity this king had long waited for, of trying his
strength against the Assyrian empire. Although Assyria was declining he did not attempt to cope with
it single-handed, but joined his attack with a revolution at Babylon, which, fortunately for him, occurred
at the time of the Assyrian monarch's death.

It is not certain who was the Assyrian monarch
at this time, but it was probably Bel-zakir-iskun, a
king whose relationship and position are unknown.

The new Assyrian monarch found himself in a
position of great danger, his dominions being attacked
on three sides; Psammitichus, king of Egypt, was
laying siege to Ashdod in the west, Babylonia on the
south had thrown off the Assyrian voke, while the

Medes, now organized into a powerful monarchy, advanced to attack him from the east.

Under these circumstances he acted with great vigour; he raised two armies; one for Babylonia, the other for Media, and committed one to the care of an officer named Nabu-pal-uzur, with orders to re-conquer Babylonia and the region of the Persian Gulf, while he himself opposed Phraortes. Nabu-pal-uzur or Nabopolassar succeeded completely in his enter-prise; he defeated the rebels, and reconquered the whole region of the south, and received from his lord in reward the title of king of Babylonia.

In the east for a time similar success appeared to attend the operations of his royal master; he drove back the Medes, and pursued them into their own country, bringing them to bay in the plain of Rhages. Here the Assyrians inflicted a crushing defeat on the Medes, and Phraortes fell in the battle. The triumph of the Assyrians was, however, short-lived, for the death of the Median king did not put an end to the war. Phraortes was succeeded by his son Vakistar, the Cyaxares of the Greeks, a man of great courage and military genius, who continued the contest with the Assyrian monarch, and expelled him from Media. Cyaxares in his turn invaded Assyria, and went up with a view of besieging Nineveh, then the capital of the country. This enterprise was put an end to by one of those remarkable floods of barbarians, which so often poured from the northern plains of Europe and Asia upon the more fertile and civilized lands of the south.

At this time, beyond the mountains of Caucasus lived a number of wandering tribes called Saci of

Scythians, who had been gradually encroaching on the south for some years. Pressing before them the Gimirri or Cimmerians, they had driven these into Asia Minor, and large bodies of the Scythians were now prepared to follow them.

The king of Assyria being now in great difficulty, surrounded by revolt and pressed by the victorious Medes, the appearance of the Scythians must have been to him most welcome. It is quite possible that he in the first place tempted these barbarians to leave their native wilds, and descend on Media, but in any case they came in time to save the existence of the Assyrian empire.

According to Herodotus the Scythians crossed the Caucasus in great numbers, and invaded Media, under the conduct of a leader named Madyas; and Cyaxares turning to encounter them was defeated and compelled to submit to their dominion. Hordes of Scythians now overran Media, Assyria, and Syria, and they are said to have advanced to Askelon and burned the temple of Venus there. Psammitichus went out and met these barbarians, and by rich presents tempted them to turn aside and not invade Egypt.

During the time of the Scythian invasion the Assyrian king retained his nominal sovereignty, but his new allies, according to the accounts which have come down to us, did little but plunder and ravage in every direction.

Bel-zakir-iskun, king of Assyria, has left very few memorials, the principal being some fragments of memorial cylinders from Nineveh; it appears from these that he made some additions to the temples at Nineveh; in these inscriptions he states that the gods had given him the victory over all his enemies, but he goes into no details of his reign.

It is probable that the rule of Bel-zakir-iskun was short, and he was succeeded by Assur-ebil-ili, who was son of Assur-bani-pal. This monarch restored the temple of Nebo at the city of Calah, called Bit-sidda, and he bears the usual grand titles of the Assyrian monarchs, but it is probable that his power was limited and his empire shorn of its ancient grandeur. Assur-ebil-ili is supposed to have been the Saracus of the Greeks, under whom the Assyrian monarchy was destroyed.

The dominion of the Scythians lasted many years, and riot and luxury gradually reduced their forces, until tired of their yoke the chiefs of Asia resolved to get rid of their presence. According to the account of Herodotus, Cyaxares having invited the principal chiefs to a banquet put them to death, and afterwards drove out their followers.

During about fifteen years, Nabopolassar had been consolidating his power at Babylon, when conceiving the project of overthrowing the feeble Assyrian empire, he entered into a controversy with the king of Assyria, claiming new rights as a pretext for revolting and making war on his former master.

About B.C. 610 he entered into an alliance with Necho, king of Egypt, and sending to Cyaxares, who had just expelled the Scythians, he asked the hand of Amuhia or Amytis, daughter of the Median monarch, for his eldest son Nabu-kudur-uzur (Nebuchadnezzar), to cement an alliance between the two powers; and proposed that they should together attack the Assyrian empire.

These propositions were readily agreed to by Cyaxares, who remembered his father's defeat and death,
his own expedition to Assyria, and the injuries he
and his people had suffered at the hands of the
Scythians, and it was evident that the coming war
would be one of great bitterness. The king of Armenia, whose ancestors had always been hostile to
Assyria, joined the league; and the Ninevite monarch
was surrounded on all sides by enemies.

The confederates marched out about B.C. 609.
Necho, king of Egypt, determined on passing through
Judah, but Josiah king of Judah, who remained
faithful in his allegiance to Assyria, resolved to bar
his way, and brought out his army to Megiddo.
Necho sent to Josiah and tried to dissuade him from
this, but the king of Judah refused to listen, and
consequently Necho attacked his army at Megiddo
and routed it, Josiah himself being mortally wounded
in the battle. As soon as he had cleared his path,
Necho at once pushed on to join in the attack on
the Assyrian empire.

At this time the great centre of the trade between
the west and Nineveh, and the place where the
Euphrates was generally crossed, was Karchemesh,
now an Assyrian fortress, the centre of a province,
and the band which connected Assyria with Syria.
For this point Necho made, and attacking Karchemesh captured it and occupied it with his army,
severing almost at a blow the Assyrian territory.
All the country west of the Euphrates now fell to
Necho, who fixed his court at Riblah in the land
of Hamath, and exercising his power as Suzerain

deposed Jehoahaz king of Judah, and set up in his
place his brother Jehoiakim, placing on the country
a tribute of 100 talents of silver and a talent of
gold. The country between the river Euphrates and
the Mediterranean remained under the power of
Necho until his defeat by Nebuchadnezzar.

The siege of the city of Nineveh was carried on
principally by the Medes and Babylonians; the details
have not been handed down by any reliable authority,
but it is probable that the accounts given by ancient
authors are partly true, and they are given here
because we have at present no better authorities.

Nabopolassar, the Babylonian monarch, and the
Arabians advanced from the south; the Medes under
Cyaxares accompanied by the Persians and Ar-
menians marched from the east: and all invaded
Assyria, overrunning the greater part of the country.

Their united forces are said to have been defeated
three times, but on the arrival of a new contingent
from the east the tide of fortune turned and Shalman, brother of the king of Assyria, was killed, and
the Assyrian army routed. The Assyrian monarch
now shut himself up in Nineveh, and the allies besieged the cities in that vicinity.

The fate of most of these is unknown; the siege
of Nineveh however is said to have lasted over two
years; the walls, which were one hundred feet high and
fifty feet thick, keeping out the enemy until one
spring there was an enormous rise of the Tigris,
and the flood carried away a considerable portion of
the wall of the city.[1] The Assyrian monarch, foreseeing the fall of the capital, now gathered his wives

[1] Compare Nahum i. 8.

and all his valuables in the palace and set the building in flames.

On the subsiding of the river, the besieging host entered the city by the breach the water had made. Nineveh was thus taken, its palaces and temples destroyed, and its people carried into captivity.

Assyria was now divided between the conquerors. Necho for the present held the west of the Euphrates, while the bulk of the country went to Babylonia, the northern mountainous region being annexed to Media.

The conquerors however soon quarrelled over the spoil, and B.C. 605 Nabopolassar sent his son Nebuchadnezzar to attack Pharaoh Necho, and the young prince coming up with the Egyptian army at Karchemesh, routed it and expelled Necho from Syria.

Assyria now ceased to have a separate existence, and was for the most part merged into Babylonia. Of its history we now know nothing until after the empire of the east had passed from Babylonia to Persia, when, somewhere about B.C. 520, Assyria joined Armenia and Media in revolting against Darius Hystaspes, under a leader named Phraortes, who called himself Xathrites, a descendant of Cyaxares. Vomises, a general of Darius, fought a battle with the rebels at the town of Achitu in Assyria. Subsequently another Median rebel was impaled at the city of Arbela in Assyria.

After this Assyria is scarcely mentioned except by travellers and historians; its cities decayed, its people dwindled away, and its history and language were lost, until revived in our own day by the explorations of Botta, Layard, Rawlinson, and others.

CLARENDON PRESS, OXFORD.
For the Society for Promoting Christian Knowledge.

www.ingramcontent.com/pod-product-compliance
Ingram Content Group UK Ltd.
Pitfield, Milton Keynes, MK11 3LW, UK
UKHW012344130625
459647UK00009B/519